Tales from the Red Sox Dugout

by
Jim Prime
with Bill Nowlin

Illustrations
by Bob Jackson

Sports Publishing Inc.
www.SportsPublishingInc.com

Director of production: Susan M. McKinney
Book design, project manager: Jennifer L. Polson
Book layout: Michelle R. Dressen
Cover design: Julie L. Denzer

ISBN: 1-58382-054-x

Printed in the United States of America.

Sports Publishing Inc.
804 North Neil
Champaign, IL 61820
www.SportsPublishingInc.com

To Glenna, Catherine and Jeffrey, my wonderful family, who put up with and even encourage my Red Sox addiction. Bill and I both offer a special tip of the cap to one of the most gracious ladies we have ever had the privilege to meet: the Queen of Fenway Park and the Red Sox's foremost fan, Lib Dooley.

ACKNOWLEDGMENTS

The Boston Red Sox inspire people to talk, often with great eloquence and always with great passion. People from all walks of life enjoy sharing their stories about this colorful team. Some of the people who helped, encouraged and/or inspired me in the writing of *Tales From the Red Sox Dugout* are: Tom Bast, Dr. Philip Belitsky, Dave Canton, Peter Cornu, Maureen Cronin, Nomar Garciaparra, Victor Garciaparra, Dick Gernert, Paul Gleason, Dabney Coleman, Bob Jackson, Bill Lee, Mickey McDermott, Bill Nowlin, Mel Parnell, Glenna Prime, Catherine Prime, Ben Robicheau, Sam Snead, Virgil Trucks, Mickey Vernon, Bill Wilder, Karen Wilder and Ted Williams. I thank them all. A special thank-you to my son Jeffrey, whose intimate knowledge of computers was instrumental in the writing of this book. Thanks, Jeff! —JHP

Bill Nowlin would like to extend his thanks to: Walter Cherniak, Jr., Bill Consolo, Maureen Cronin, Kate Gordon, Mike Ipavec, Ted Lepcio, Pedro Martinez, Slade Mead, Steve Mastroyin, Lou Merloni, Eddie Pellagrini, Paul Penta, Johnny Pesky, Kevin Shea, Bob Stanley, John Valentin, Charlie Wagner, Gary Williams, Brian Wilson, Janet Zauchin, and Tony, a waiter at Valbella's in Greenwich, Connecticut.

CONTENTS

Luis Aparicio 5
Don Baylor 7
Rod Beck 8
Dennis "The Menace" Bennett 10
Moe Berg 11
Wade Boggs 13
Dennis "Oil Can" Boyd 15
Darren Bragg 16
Bill Buckner 17
Don Buddin 17
Rick Burleson 19
Bernie Carbo 19
Roger Clemens 20
Tony Conigliaro 22
Gene Conley 25
Joe Cronin 26
Ray Culp 27
Dom DiMaggio 28
Bobby Doerr 29
Walt Dropo 30
Dwight Evans 32
Sherm Feller 33
The Ferrell Brothers, Wes and Rick 34
Dave "Boo" Ferriss 35
Carlton Fisk 36
Jimmie Foxx 38
Nomar Garciaparra 41
Dick Gernert 49
Billy Goodman 50
Mike Greenwell 52
Lefty Grove 52
Carroll Hardy 53
Tommy Harper 54
Ken Harrelson 54
Dave (Hendu) Henderson 55

Butch Hobson 56
Harry Hooper 56
Ralph Houk 57
Jackie Jensen 58
Smead Jolley 59
Jack Kramer 60
Bill Lee 61
The World According to Chairman Lee 64
Jim Lonborg 67
Sparky Lyle 68
Fred Lynn 68
Steve Lyons 70
Frank Malzone 71
Pedro Martinez 71
Mickey McDermott 77
Sam Mele 84
Lou Merloni 85
Ed Morris 86
Trot Nixon 86
Troy O'Leary 87
Johnny Orlando 88
Mel Parnell 88
Johnny Pesky 90
Rico Petrocelli 92
Jimmy Piersall 93
Dick Radatz 96
Jim Rice 97
Red Ruffing 99
Babe Ruth 100
Ray Scarborough 103
George Scott 104
Eddie Shore 106
Tris Speaker 107
Tracy Stallard 108
Bob Stanley 109
Stealing Home 110
Vern Stephens 112
Dick Stuart 112
George Thomas 115
Luis Tiant 116
John Valentin 120

Mo Vaughn 123
Mickey Vernon 124
"Broadway" Charlie Wagner 125
John Wasdin 127
Sammy White 127
Dick Williams 129
Ted Williams 129
Ted's Philadelphia Story 145
Jim Willoughby 149
Smoky Joe Wood 150
Carl Yastrzemski 151
Tom Yawkey 159
Rudy York 162
Cy Young 163
Matt Young 165
Norm Zauchin 165
Don Zimmer 166
Bibliography 169

Introduction

It isn't much of an exaggeration to say that the history of the Boston Red Sox is the history of baseball. Born in 1901, the Boston franchise was a founding member of the American League. The first modern World Series was played in 1903 between the Boston Pilgrims, as they were then known, and the Pittsburgh Pirates, with the Boston nine emerging victorious. Rechristened the Red Sox, they won again in 1912, 1915, and 1916. In 1918, the First World War ended, a young Boston pitcher named Babe Ruth led the American League with 11 homers (and compiled a 13-7 record on the pitching mound), Ted Williams was born, and the Sox won their fifth World Series. Then, just when it was beginning to look as if the 20th century belonged to the Boston Red Sox, Ruth was sold to the hated New York Yankees. Eight decades later, the annual New England cry of "Wait 'til next year!" has been replaced with "Maybe next millennium!"

Despite the extended championship drought, it can be argued that the Bosox showcased the greatest practitioners of the two basic facets of the game: hitting and pitching. They boasted Ted Williams, whose name will forever be synonymous with the science of hitting, and Cy Young, the man permanently identified with excellence in the art of pitching. Of course Babe Ruth, the personification of baseball around the world, perfected both skills at Fenway before a carpet-bagging New Yorker named Harry Frazee sold him to the Yankees in order to finance a Broadway production of *No, No, Nanette.* Frazee failed to realize that the real drama and melodrama was to be found with his Red Sox. The rise of Ruth as a bona fide Boston star and his eventual sale to the Yankees sums up the Red Sox saga—blessed and cursed in equal measure. Blessed with wonderful heroes and unforgettable heroics; cursed with bad luck and squandered opportunities.

All this makes the Red Sox more than just an American institution; it makes them a beloved team. You can't say that about many multimillion dollar corporations. You certainly can't say it about the Yankees: maybe the Mets; the Cubs and the old Brooklyn Dodgers, certainly; but never the Yanks. Teams don't become beloved strictly by fielding excellent teams; nor do they achieve this status by being just plain bad. Elements of both are necessary. There must be a core of greatness—tempered with comedic relief and at least one tragic flaw. The Red Sox have had stars, heroes and anti-heroes in abundance. Like Sisyphus, the Sox keep pushing the rock up the mountain—only to have it roll right down again. They have shown periodic flashes of brilliance—only to fall just short, often in dramatic style. For every Ted Williams hitting a home run in his last at-bat, there is a Bill Buckner with the ball going through his legs. For every Carlton Fisk game-winning home run, there is the specter of Bucky Dent's devastating 1978 playoff homer. For every 1967 Impossible Dream, there is the very real nightmare of the 1986 "One Strike Away" World Series.

The Red Sox image is a curious mix of vulnerability, humanity, and humor. America loves underdogs, and the Sox are the perpetual underdog. As such, they are more convincing in the role of "America's Team" than the media-hyped and image-conscious Atlanta Braves or Yankees.

This book is meant to capture the many sides of the Boston Red Sox: the humor, the brilliance, the humanity, and the countless eccentricities that make them what they are. Anyone who has followed the Red Sox even casually has a favorite story about this team.

My own favorite anecdote about the Red Sox? In the early '80s, I wrote a number of articles on Ted Williams and in 1995 co-authored a book with Williams, entitled *Ted Williams' Hit List*, a ranking of the greatest hitters in baseball history. As a result of all this, Ted's name became a household word in our home. In 1983, I visited Fenway Park to see a game between the Red Sox and Kansas City Royals. By the 3rd inning, my three-year-old daughter Catherine had dozed off in the hot August sun just as Carl Yastrzemski launched a long homer into the bleachers. Abruptly awakened by the cheers, Catherine joined in the spirit if not the substance of the celebration. "Hooray for Ted Williams!" she said. Although those words had almost certainly not been uttered at Fenway since September 26, 1960, they sounded not at all out of place. Fans around us seemed to understand and smiled approvingly, as if those unspoken words had been rattling through Fenway Park for decades and needed only a naïve child to give voice to them. The Red Sox are like that—a great, unfinished novel with lots of intriguing characters. To get the full impact of what happens in any one chapter, you should have a working knowledge of previous chapters. The effect is cumulative. The Red Sox are connected to the past yet timeless, and what happened in 1939 or 1960 still means something today.

Red Sox fans know that for good or for bad they are cheering for an American original; the most fascinating franchise in professional sports. I hope the stories in this book help to capture some of their magic for you.

–Jim Prime

Luis Aparicio

I t was 1971, and Red Sox shortstop Luis Aparicio was mired in the worst slump of his long and distinguished major-league career. He had been held hitless for 11 games and 44 at-bats. On June 1, he singled, a small oasis in a desert of batting futility, but then went hitless for two more games and was now 1-for-55. On June 4, he received a note from President Richard Nixon, who wrote: "In my own career, I have experienced long periods when I couldn't seem to get a hit, regardless of how hard I tried, but in the end, I was able to hit a home run." Inspired by the President's support, the 37-year-old Aparicio went out that day and earned a standing ovation for knocking in two runs. His slump was over. As for Nixon, his next slump would prove to be his last.

O n the final day of the 1971 season, Luis was preparing to head back to Venezuela. Something of a fashion plate, he wore his Oleg Cassini jacket, his Oleg Cassini pants and his Oleg Cassini shoes to the ballpark. He had already sent the rest of his luggage to the airport, and all he had was his ticket, his uniform and the elegant clothes on his back. Carl Yastrzemski, a brutal practical joker who wasn't playing that day, went to the clubhouse in the late innings of the game and cut his pants at the knees, cut the lapels off his jacket, cut his tie in half and nailed his shoes to the hardwood floor. Luis was forced to make his way back home in borrowed Bermuda shorts.

Luis Aparicio

Don Baylor

Don Baylor was a stylish hitter, an intelligent ballplayer, a born leader with fire in his belly—and a winner. He came to the Red Sox late in his career, bringing that winning tradition with him. The best designated hitter in baseball at the time, he became the first player to reach the World Series in three consecutive seasons for three different teams—the 1986 Red Sox, the 1987 Minnesota Twins and the 1988 Oakland Athletics. Baylor was fearless. He'd stand close to the plate and defy pitchers to throw at him, yelling as a reliever strode to the mound: "You're the guy I've been waiting for since batting practice!" Often they obliged, making Baylor number one on the all-time hit-by-pitch list. Baylor was hit by a season-record 35 pitches in 1986 and took one for the team a total of 267 times in his career. Ouch!

When Baylor came to the Red Sox in 1986 from the New York Yankees, Yankee owner George Steinbrenner predicted that the aging, 36-year-old slugger's bat would be "dead by August." August came, and Baylor hit seven home runs and drove in 14 runs. Steinbrenner later apologized, claiming he had been misquoted. Actually it was his Yankees that were on life support.

B aylor was perhaps best known for the Kangaroo Courts he established. The idea was to have some fun while at the same time keeping players loose and boosting morale. Baylor was the judge, and fines could be imposed for almost any on-field "infraction." Some players, of course, were repeat offenders. Steve "Psycho" Lyons was fined for fraternizing with opposing players, socializing with fans, being on the field without his cap and so on. When Lyons was traded from the Red Sox, Baylor lamented: "There goes half our Kangaroo Court fund."

Rod Beck

I t may have been the longest trip in from the bullpen in the history of baseball. He had never been to Boston, let alone Fenway Park, but when reliever Rod Beck came over to the Red Sox in a trade with the National League's Chicago Cubs in the middle of the '99 stretch drive, the long-haired, mustachioed right-hander was immediately pressed into action. Arriving at Fenway after a six-hour flight from California followed by a stressful 40-minute cab ride from the airport, the Sox's brand new closer had scarcely located the bullpen when he was called in against the Kansas City Royals in the

Rod Beck

ninth inning. "The Red Sox fans gave him a great ovation," said Nomar Garciaparra. "I mean, he was with the Cubs—in the other league—but they still knew how good he is, and they give him a great reception. It just shows how knowledgeable Boston fans are." First baseman Mike Stanley literally had to introduce himself to Beck during the meeting at the mound: "How you doing, Rod? Welcome to the Red Sox. I'm Mike Stanley, and I'll be your first baseman today. " Catcher Jason Varitek extended his hand in greeting. "Hi, I'm Jason Varitek," he said. "What do ya got?" Despite his long trip, Beck's first outing was successful. He threw eleven pitches and recorded his first save for the Red Sox. "I'd never met him either," recalls Garciaparra, "but

I figured I'd introduce myself after the game." In his initial eight appearances in a Sox uniform he was almost untouchable, allowing just four hits in his first 10 pressure-packed innings of work.

Dennis "The Menace" Bennett

Pitcher Dennis Bennett used to carry five guns with him on road trips. One evening, he got into a heated argument with roommate Lee "Mad Dog" Thomas over who should get up to turn out the light in their room. Players in the next room overheard the angry shouts and then were startled by a loud gunshot. Expecting the worst, the players rushed to the scene of the mayhem, passing a rapidly retreating Thomas in the hallway. When they reached Bennett's room, they discovered that he had solved the dispute by shooting out the light with his pistol.

Lacking sufficient money for a plane ticket to a teammate's wedding, Bennett enlisted the help of a stewardess friend and stowed away on a cross-country flight. Giving new meaning to the term "relief pitcher," Bennett remained in one of the plane's toilets, protected by a sign that read "Out of Service."

Moe Berg

Red Sox catcher Moe Berg was a spy. No, not just another one of those guys who gets to second base and tries to steal the catcher's signs in order to relay them to the batter—although had he *reached* second more often, he doubtless would have become quite adept at that too. Berg was a real spy for the U.S. during World War II.

In 1934, Berg visited Japan as part of an All-Star barnstorming tour. With a puny .251 average, Berg's credentials for such a trip paled beside those of teammates such as Ruth and Gehrig. Why then was he chosen? While there he reportedly took a large number of photographs which years later were used by U.S. intelligence to plan air attacks on Tokyo.

It was once said of Berg: "He could speak a dozen languages and couldn't hit in any of them." During a 15-year career, he compiled a modest .243 batting average, with just six home runs.

Moe Berg

Prior to departure for the series of games in Japan, Babe Ruth asked Berg: "You're such a brilliant linguist; do you speak Japanese?" The catcher replied that he did not. After two weeks on the high seas, the ship carrying the baseball stars arrived in Japan. As they were disembarking, Berg engaged a welcoming committee in animated conversation—in apparently fluent Japanese. Ruth was astounded. "I thought you didn't speak

Japanese," he said. "That was two weeks ago," Berg replied.

Wade Boggs

Ballplayers are a superstitious lot; none more so than former Red Sox third baseman Wade Boggs. Boggs was known for drawing Hebrew letters in the batter's box for luck. He also had a fixation with the numbers 7 and 17. He took his wind sprints at 7:17 each evening (this was before the days of the 7:05 start) and in 1984 asked the Red Sox for the precise sum of $717,000. Boggs' major quirk was a daily diet of chicken, prepared one of fifty different ways. His wife Debbie was so inspired that she even went so far as to author a cookbook entitled *Fowl Tips*.

During the 1985 season, Boggs batted .368 and showed his great patience as a hitter. He popped up just three times in 653 at-bats, and two of those were foul. During that same season, he compiled 240 hits, and 124 of those came with two strikes on him—something that would make Ted "a walk is as good as a hit" Williams smile. Boggs swung at and missed a grand

Wade Boggs

total of one first pitch all season long. In 1987, he hit a robust .390 with the count at 0 and 2.

Boggs' days with the Red Sox were not without controversy. In 1989, a very public scandal involving Margo Adams tarnished his image and threatened to scuttle his marriage, and for a while he was forced to endure brutal heckling both at home and on the road. His season batting average fell from .366 the previous year to a slightly more earthly .330, and for the first time in recent memory he failed to capture the batting title. Boggs endured however, and when he retired at the end of the 1999 campaign with a .328 average and 3010 hits, he was a sure bet for a spot in baseball's Hall of Fame. Defying those who dismiss him as a doubles hitter, his 3000th hit was a 372-foot home run.

Dennis "Oil Can" Boyd

"I sometimes act like I'm from another planet."
–Dennis "Oil Can" Boyd

Dennis Boyd hailed from Meridian, Mississippi, the home of legendary Satchel Paige and—because he is black, wiry, countrified, loves to talk and has a colorful nickname—many people thought of him as the reincarnation of Satch. In some parts of the south, beer is known as "oil," and since Boyd loved beer as a teenager, he was given the name Oil Can. The son of an ex-Negro League star, the Can even kept a picture of Paige in his locker. Boyd did not share Satch's laid-back philosophy, however. He had a temper. When he was left off the 1985 All-Star team by manager Sparky Anderson, he was upset. When he was left off by Dick Howser in 1986, he went ballistic, throwing a tantrum in the Red Sox dressing room and verbally abusing several teammates. He was suspended for three days without pay.

Darren Bragg

Trying desperately to beat the throw from short-stop, Darren Bragg slid headfirst into first base on a close play at Fenway. The only problem was that he started his slide too soon and ended up several feet short of his goal. The next day, during batting practice, his Red Sox teammates decided to help him out. "We put another base 10 feet in front of the actual bag," said Nomar Garciaparra. "Right where he ended up. We said, this is Darren Bragg's first base. He plays by different rules. We told him if first base were right here, you would have been safe."

Bill Buckner

Game Six of the 1986 World Series was hardly a laugh riot for Red Sox fans. It was as if Wile E. Coyote had finally caught the tasty but elusive Roadrunner, only to have the annoying little creature escape once again from the boiling pot. Beep! Beep! The '86 Red Sox came within one pitch of a World Series championship and let it slip through their hands—or more accurately, through Bill Buckner's legs. (Bleep! Bleep!) The humor that the game does present is of the darkest possible variety. Before the game, Sox manager John McNamara was asked who would start at first base, Buckner or Don Baylor. His reply: "Probably Buckner. He was hobbling at one hundred percent today." Buckner later let a ground ball go through his legs, resulting in the most devastating loss in Sox history. He later moved to Idaho to escape his infamy.

Don Buddin

Don Buddin had a reputation as an erratic fielder. In 1956, '58 and '59, the clean-cut Red Sox shortstop led the American League in double plays. Unfor-

Bill Buckner

tunately, in two of those years he also topped the league in errors. Former Boston writer and radio personality Clif Keane once incurred Buddin's wrath by suggesting in print that he should have "E-6" as his license plate.

Rick Burleson

Announcer Joe Garagiola once described shortstop "Rooster" Burleson as follows: "He's even-tempered. He comes to the ballpark mad, and he stays that way."

Bernie Carbo

"Bernie was baseball's Forrest Gump." – Bill Lee

Bernie Carbo was an unorthodox ballplayer who traveled with a stuffed gorilla named Mighty Joe Young who he occasionally ordered for in restaurants. Bernie Carbo's chief claim to fame was the clutch home run that he hit in Game Six of the 1975 World Series, a contest that many consider the greatest ever played. With two strikes, and the Red Sox down 6-3 in the bottom of the eighth, Carbo hit a three-run homer off ace Cincinnati reliever Rawly Eastwick to tie the game. The unlikely home run set the stage for Carlton Fisk's dramatic game-winning homer in the bottom of the 12th inning.

I n 1977, Carbo slugged a bases-loaded homer against Seattle Mariners' left-hander Mike Kekich. After the game, reporters gathered around his locker to ask him about the grand slam. "Grand slam?" said a startled Carbo, who had failed to notice that the bases were loaded while he was at bat. Another reporter asked when he had last homered off a southpaw pitcher. Carbo laughed. "Now I know you're pulling my leg, because he was a right-handed pitcher," he said confidently. "(Red Sox manager Don) Zimmer would never let me hit against a left-hander with the bases loaded."

W hen Carbo was sold to Cleveland in 1978, his best friend Bill Lee went on an unofficial strike. He confronted his manager Don Zimmer. "I thought you said that Bernie was like a son to you?" said Lee. "Well, I've got news for you; you don't trade your son to Cleveland."

Roger Clemens

R ocket Roger Clemens has had some memorable days on the mound for the Red Sox, but none

Roger Clemens

greater than the day in May of 1986 when he set a new major-league record by striking out 20 Seattle Mariners. At that point, the record for a nine-inning game was 19, shared by Steve Carlton, Nolan Ryan and Tom Seaver. In the contest, Clemens threw 138 pitches—97 of them strikes. Of the 97 strikes only 29 were sullied by contact with wood, and 19 of those were foul balls. In baseball's version of "float like a butterfly and sting like a bee," he painted the corners like an artist and threw inside like a hired assassin. What makes

Clemens' achievement even more amazing was the fact that just eight months earlier he had undergone shoulder surgery. As the strikeout totals continued to build, the Fenway faithful reacted enthusiastically when first baseman Mike Easler dropped a foul ball, allowing Clemens to notch yet another K. Clemens went on to earn American League MVP honors and capture the Cy Young award.

The names of Clemens' kids all begin with K—the baseball symbol for strikeout. For the record, they are Koby, Kory, Kacy and Kody. Klever!

Tony Conigliaro
"He was baseball's JFK."–Dick Johnson

It was the kind of debut that every kid dreams about. Just two years out of St. Mary's High School in Lynn, Massachusetts, 19-year-old rookie right fielder Tony Conigliaro stepped into the batter's box and homered off Chicago's Joel Horlen on the first pitch thrown to him at Fenway Park. One writer suggested that it was the fastest start by anyone in town "since Paul Revere beat the British out of the gate." It was 1964, and the home opener was a special game to benefit the planned

John F. Kennedy Memorial Library. Conigliaro was performing before a celebrity-filled crowd that included Bobby and Teddy Kennedy, the governor of Massachusetts, Boston's mayor, boxers Jack Dempsey and Gene Tunney, Cardinal Cushing, the Harvard University band and an impressive array of film stars, including Carol Channing. Despite missing more than 50 games due to injury, Conigliaro, with a swing ideally suited to Fenway, poked 24 home runs over the Green Monster while hitting at a .290 clip. In his sophomore year, he became baseball's youngest home run king, leading the American League with 32 at the age of 20. He added 28 more in 1966, but both the production and the injury were harbingers of things to come.

There have been two great tragedies in Red Sox history, both involving local Boston boys with matinee-idol good looks and seemingly limitless futures. The first involved the Golden Greek, Harry Agganis, who died tragically in 1953 at the age of 23. The second of the Greco-Roman tragedies came more than a decade later on August 18, 1967, a steamy night in the midst of one of the hottest and most memorable pennant races in American League history. Hometown hero Tony Conigliaro was hit in the head by a fastball thrown by California Angels pitcher Jack Hamilton. The blow almost killed him and he was never the same again. He had 20 home runs at the time of his beaning.

R ed Sox manager Darrell Johnson once spied Conigliaro coming out of a nightclub after curfew. Tony C insisted that he had only ducked into the establishment to get directions to Midnight Mass.

B efore "vanity plates" were commonplace, the governor of Massachusetts issued a set of personalized plates to Conigliaro in recognition of the great rookie season the hometown boy had put together. The plates bore only the letters "T.C." Unfortunately, some overzealous fans decided that the plates would make a nice souvenir and stole them, bumpers and all.

N ew England fans loved Tony C. Following his beaning, his eyesight took a long time to come back and never did return completely. After striking out four times in one game, he complained about fans wearing white shirts in the bleacher triangle. He said the glare off the shirts made it difficult to see the ball and created a dangerous situation for hitters, and proposed that fans sitting in that area be given green or blue vests to wear during the game. The Red Sox responded, posting a sign which read: "Dear Patron, please do not sit in green seat section unless you are wearing dark-colored clothing. Conig thanks you. Management thanks you." Fans entering the seats in this area were given cards stating: "You are now an official member of Conig's Corner. The Red Sox and Tony C appreciate your cooperation in helping to provide a good hitting background."

Gene Conley

Following a game at Yankee Stadium in July 1962, losing pitcher Gene Conley and teammate Pumpsie Green, the first black man to play for the Red Sox, were traveling back to the hotel in the team bus. When the bus became trapped in a New York traffic jam, Conley and Green jumped ship and disappeared into the crowd. They checked into a hotel and proceeded to get inebriated. At least one of the two defectors then seems to have undergone a profound religious experience. Green's pilgrimage was back to the Red Sox, but Conley headed for the airport with every intention of flying to Israel "to get nearer to God." A ticket agent pointed out that he had no passport, and he sheepishly returned to the Boston fold. Both were fined by owner Tom Yawkey, and Green was later banished to the then-lowly New York Mets.

Someone once spotted Gene Conley alone and crying in a church. The concerned observer asked him if he had lost a loved one. "Yes," he sobbed. "My fastball."

In addition to being something of a flake, Red Sox pitcher Gene Conley was an all-around athlete and no stranger to the thrill of victory. Before coming to the Red Sox, he was a member of the 1957 World Series champion Milwaukee Braves. He also performed with the NBA champion Boston Celtics of 1959, 1960 and 1961.

Joe Cronin

In a 1935 game against Cleveland at Fenway Park, Red Sox shortstop Joe Cronin (later to become Red Sox manager and eventually American League president) came to bat with none out, the bases loaded and the Red Sox down by a 5-3 count. Cronin drove a vicious line drive down the third base line that handcuffed Indians third baseman Odell "Bad News" Hale.

The ball struck him in the forehead and ricocheted to shortstop William Knickerbocker for the first out. Knickerbocker relayed it to second baseman Billy Werber to get the runner, and Werber threw it to first baseman Hal Trosky to complete the triple play. Three outs—possibly four if you include Hale, who was nearly out cold.

Ray Culp

Red Sox pitcher Ray Culp was once hit in the head by a line drive off the bat of Detroit Tigers strongman Willie Horton. The ball bounced high into the air toward center field, where Reggie Smith made a diving catch for the second out of the inning. Culp hung in there and retired the next batter to end the game. When questioned later about the strange play, Culp's straight-faced reply was: "Don't ever tell me I don't know where to play hitters."

Dom DiMaggio

"Dom could do it all. He ran the bases like a gazelle, he played a flawless center field, and he possessed a rifle-arm." –Ted Williams

Dom DiMaggio may well be the best player not in the Hall of Fame. According to a song that was popular in New England but less so in New York: "He's better than his brother Joe; Dominic DiMaggio!" Well, probably not. But Dom DiMaggio was still pretty darn good. The Little Professor, so called because of the spectacles he sported, was one of the premier center fielders in baseball history, and no less an authority than Ted Williams has actively campaigned for his induction into the Hall of Fame. Little wonder. DiMaggio was a table-setter for Ted, who feasted on AL pitching and drove Dom home more often than Morgan Freeman chauffeured Miss Daisy in that direction.

Dom's brother Joe holds the major-league-record hitting streak of 56, but in 1949, Dom set the Red Sox record by hitting safely in 34 consecutive games. Who knows how much further he might have gone had his hard line drive off Yankee pitcher Vic Raschi not been snagged by another agile center fielder. The center fielder's name? Joseph DiMaggio. Blood may be thicker than water but not where baseball is concerned. The headline in a Boston paper the next day screamed: JOE DIMAGGIO'S CATCH STOPS BROTHER'S STREAK. Explaining the catch to Dom after the game, the Yankee Clipper was almost apologetic. "If I had let the ball go through, it would have hit me right between the eyes," he said.

DiMaggio was a true gentleman both on and off the field. A home plate umpire once called him out on some very borderline strikes. As always, DiMaggio kept his composure and didn't turn around to confront the man in blue. When he got back to the dugout, he rested for a moment with his knee on the top step, then removed his glasses and began methodically wiping them off. He gazed steadily out at the umpire and said in a calm, almost meditative voice: "I have never witnessed such incompetence in all my life." Manager Joe McCarthy, accustomed to slightly saltier language from his ballplayers, fell off the bench laughing.

Bobby Doerr

"Bobby Doerr is one of the very few who played this game hard and came out of it with no enemies." – Tommy Henrich

R ed Sox second baseman Bobby Doerr once handled 414 fielding chances flawlessly before committing an error—a streak that encompassed almost three months. But Doerr was much more than just another good-field, no-hit infielder. His hitting credentials were equally impressive. Although known for his ability to get on base for Ted Williams and other Red Sox big guns, Doerr also hit 223 lifetime home runs and drove in 1,247. His versatility at the plate and in the field carried him all the way to baseball's Hall of Fame.

Walt Dropo

W alt Dropo's former roommate was Red Sox south-paw Mickey McDermott. McDermott was 15 years old and 138 pounds soaking wet when the 6'5", 240-pound rookie first knocked on his door and introduced himself. "He was the biggest son of a bitch I ever saw in my life. I thought that the Ringling Brothers Circus truck must have broken down and Garantua was rooming with me. I said: 'You got any bananas with you?' I said: 'Hey Moose, when you die leave your head to the Elks Club so they can put antlers on it.' " Dropo went on to capture the AL Rookie of the Year award on the strength of 34 homers, a .322 average and 144 RBIs.

Walt Dropo

Red Sox pitcher and part-time singer Mickey McDermott became Dropo's best friend on the Red Sox. One winter evening McDermott was performing in a Boston nightclub when Dropo arrived with a young lady on each arm. In order to make an impression on the lovely young things, Dropo had arranged for a table near the stage. Spotting his teammate, McDermott said: "Ladies and gentlemen, sitting in the front row is the great first baseman for the Boston Red Sox, Mr. Walter Dropo." Dropo glowed as he acknowledged the applause from the audience. "In fact," continued McDermott, "he's so good that they named a town here in Massachusetts after him. It's called Marblehead."

Dwight Evans

Every Red Sox fan worth his salt remembers Carlton Fisk's dramatic game-winning homer in Game Six of the 1975 World Series. Without the heroics of right fielder Dwight Evans, there would probably have been no opportunity for such heroics. Evans' one-handed stab of Joe Morgan's apparent home run in the 11th inning kept the Red Sox's hopes alive. Evans whirled and threw a strike to double up baserunner Ken Griffey Sr. for the third out, setting the stage for Fisk.

When Evans first came up to the Red Sox, Bill Lee was so impressed that he told reporters that the rookie might be the next DiMaggio. Two Boston radio hosts known for their negative approach to sports reportage commented: "Yeah, he'll be Vince DiMaggio."

In 1986, a season that was to become infamous in Red Sox history, Dwight Evans swung at the very first offering of the campaign and drove it out of the ballpark—the only time that it had been done. Asked about it after the game, Evans was not impressed. "No big deal," he said. "We lost."

Sherm Feller

Red Sox public address announcer Sherm Feller once intoned: "Will the fans in center field please remove their clothes?" After a brief pause, and to the delight of the large bleacher population, he quickly added: "From the railing."

On July 20, 1969, Sherm Feller informed a large throng at Fenway Park that Neil Armstrong had made history by setting foot on the moon. The effect on the crowd was stunning as patrons discussed the milestone event with their friends. The umpire finally called time. Baltimore Orioles' future Hall of Fame third baseman Brooks Robinson had not heard the announcement and approached the plate ready to hit. When the umpire gave him the news, he spontaneously dropped his bat and began to applaud the feat. Someone in the crowd started to sing "God Bless America," and soon, the whole ballpark was joining in the patriotic chorus.

The Ferrell Brothers—Wes and Rick

One of the great brother combinations in Red Sox history was Wes and Rick Ferrell. Rick was a catcher who made it to the Hall of Fame. Wes was a pitcher who once won 20 for the Sox, but he was also a feared hitter and actually recorded more career home runs than his brother.

Wes Ferrell had his combative side as well. One time, he was so angered by a loss that he took a pair of scissors and cut his pitching glove into pieces. Another time, he punched himself in the head twice, knocking himself against the dugout wall both times until fellow players grabbed him and restrained him. His uniforms and caps also suffered occasional severe damage.

Dave "Boo" Ferriss

"He's the only man I ever knew in baseball who never has an unkind word to say." –Johnny Pesky

According to all reports, "Boo" Ferriss was the most clean-cut person that you could ever meet; a true southern gentleman. "Boo never used profanities, and the strongest words out of his mouth were: 'Oh shuckins!' " recalls former roommate Mel Parnell. Teammates used every trick in the book to try to get him to curse but with no success. Pitcher Mickey Harris used to switch his shoes so he'd have two lefts or two rights, and on one famous occasion nailed Ferriss' spikes to the floor in front of his locker. Ferriss got dressed and then slipped into the shoes and tied the laces. When he got up and tried to walk, he promptly fell on his face. His teammates howled with laughter. If ever there was time to abandon your principles and utter a few choice oaths, that time had arrived. Instead, Ferriss looked up dolefully at his roommate Tex Hughson and in his best Mississippi drawl said: "Tex, someone done done me wrong."

In his rookie year of 1945, Ferriss had an auspicious debut. His first 10 major league pitches were balls, but he recovered and won the game—a shutout. He finished the season at 21-10 and achieved a remarkable feat, particularly for a greenhorn: he beat every team in the league the first time he faced them.

Carlton Fisk

In the year 2000, Carlton Fisk was voted into baseball's Hall of Fame in Cooperstown, largely because of his performance in Game 6 of the 1975 World Series. Fisk's 12th inning, game-winning home run at 12:33 a.m. on October 22 of that year was the most famous in Red Sox history and remains one of baseball's shining moments. Fisk hit Cincinnati pitcher Pat Darcy's first pitch directly at the left-field foul pole, using unforgettable body language to will it fair.

As a catcher, Fisk liked to challenge hitters, but Bill Lee was strictly a finesse pitcher. This led to some heated meetings on the mound. "I liked to experiment," says Lee. "I would throw a change-up when he didn't expect it, and he'd get really mad. It always embarrassed me that he could throw the ball back to me harder than I could throw it to the plate."

Carlton Fisk

Jimmie Foxx

J immie Foxx, the Red Sox slugger known throughout baseball as "Beast," had an intimidating effect on opposing pitchers. With arms like tree trunks and power to spare, he was a pitcher's worst nightmare. Yankee hurler Lefty Gomez once faced him in a key situation at Fenway. Gomez shook off the first sign from catcher Bill Dickey. He shook off the second sign and the third. Finally Dickey called time and strode purposefully to the mound. "I've gone through every pitch you have! What do you want to throw to him?" the Hall of Fame receiver demanded. "If you want to know the truth, Bill," said Gomez. "I was kind of hopin' he'd get bored and go home."

G omez once described a tremendous homer that Foxx had hit against him. "It went into the third deck at Yankee Stadium," he said with a hint of pride in his voice. "Why, you couldn't walk out there in an hour." When Yankee manager Joe McCarthy inquired about what pitch Double X had hit, the reply was: "It was the greatest pitch I ever threw—for the first 60 feet." Unfortunately, the distance to home plate is 60'6".

Jimmie Foxx

Lefty Gomez once admitted: "Jimmie Foxx could hit me at midnight with the lights out."

"Pitching to Foxx is easy," said Gomez. "I just give him my best pitch and then run to back up third base." Later in his starry career, Gomez admitted: "I'm throwing as hard as ever, but the ball isn't getting there as fast."

Jimmie Foxx was known by his Red Sox teammates as a low-ball hitter and a high-ball drinker.

In 1938, Jimmie Foxx had a banner year at the plate, winning two-thirds of baseball's Triple Crown. He led the American League with a .349 average and drove in a league best 175. In most seasons, his 50 home runs would have made him a runaway leader in that category as well, but Hank Greenberg chose that same year to hit 58. In an early season game against the St. Louis Browns that year, Foxx was running a high fever and should have been home in bed. However, because the Red Sox lineup was decimated by injuries, Foxx agreed to play. He later admitted that he was barely able to see the ball, let alone hit it. But this was Jimmie Foxx, and luckily his reputation alone was worth something. In six trips to the plate, Foxx failed to offer at a single pitch and was walked six straight times, setting a major league record in the respect category. He walked a total of 119 times that season.

Even the great Ted Williams was in awe of Foxx's brute strength: "It sounded like cherry bombs going off when Foxx hit them. Hank Greenberg hit them pretty near as far, but they didn't sound that same way. They sounded like firecrackers when Mantle and Foxx hit them. At Fenway, I remember him hitting this long, long homer over the Wall into the teeth of a gale, and I remember looking at all those muscles as he trotted around the base and shaking that huge hand of his as he crossed the plate—and feeling almost weak. I was a skinny guy anyway, and I felt weak in comparison to Jimmie Foxx."

Nomar Garciaparra

Nomar Garciaparra might just be the best thing to happen to baseball in Boston since the birth of Ted Williams. The young Red Sox shortstop is almost too good to be true. On the field, he is one of the game's brightest offensive and defensive stars. Off the field he is a poster boy for good behavior, the kind of kid you'd like to introduce to your daughter. He possesses the idealism and heroic naivete of Don Quixote and has the earning potential of Donald Trump. At the plate, Nomar has more moves than Don Juan and is more deadly than Don Corleone. Before each pitch, Nomar steps out of the box and tightens his batting gloves, adjusts his wristbands, repeatedly taps the toes of first one foot and then the other. He then whacks the bat once against his back before settling in to hit. He repeats the procedure between each pitch. But his superstitions go beyond the ball field. He listens to the same music while making his way to the ballpark—always via the same route. In the clubhouse, he invariably puts on first his right sock then the left, right stirrup, left stirrup, etc. "He'd have a hard time hitting me, "says Bill Lee of Garciaparra. "I'd make so much fun of his antics. Every time he'd come up. I'd be fixing my glove, fixing my shoes. We'd go back and forth, back and forth, and eventually the ump would call the game."

"My routine really doesn't take that long," argues Nomar. "People think it takes forever because I stand right at the plate to do it. I always keep one foot in the box. That probably stems from college—there used to be a college rule where you had to keep one foot in the batter's box or you'd get an automatic strike called against you. The toe-tapping thing and the glove tightening I've done as far back as I can remember. As a little kid, I'd tap my toes. The reason I did that was because I just liked the feeling of my toes being at the end of my shoes when I was about to exert any energy. That's basically what I'm doing when I'm tapping them —getting my toes to the end of my shoes. People ask me if my shoes were too small when I was a kid, and I say it wouldn't matter how tight my shoes were, I just liked that feeling of them being in there. That's how I started tapping my toes. I don't do any set number. I don't know if it's a timing thing or not.

"I hit and I play the game on a lot of feeling. It's important how I feel when I'm about to hit. When I step out of the box, it's important how my feet feel. The way my hands feel is just as important to me. When I pull my gloves, I'm pulling down to get my hands to the end of the gloves so that it feels tight like I have nothing on. That way I can grip the bat better. Again, there's no set number of times. I just pull them until I'm ready. Some players call time and step out of the box and walk around thinking about the previous pitch or whatever. For me it's just: Now I'm ready. Let's go. It extends to what I do even before I get to the ballpark. I truly believe that baseball is such a repetitive game. You play this game *every day* and people ask me how you get better at it. Well, you take a lot of ground balls and you take a lot of swings—over and over and over . . . and over.

"I truly believe that I get into the routine because I expect to perform well every day. I'm going up against the best every day. There's no room to slack off. People expect you to play your best every day, and so I go through a routine to prepare myself—so that I know that I'm physically and mentally ready—prepared for the game. Where I can say to myself—*OK, I'm ready!* Every day!

"I don't like having excuses. I don't want to have to make any excuse for playing bad. I played bad because of this or that. I can just say I played bad because I was horrible today, and I've got to work on it tomorrow or do something to get myself better. That's why I have a basic routine. I think I know I'm ready and I have a job to do—this is my job. People expect me to go out there and play my best. They pay their money to see that. I really feel that if I stayed away or wasn't ready or prepared, I'm really doing them a huge injustice.

"When I first entered the league, opposing players and umpires would look at me and say: "What are you doing?" They might make comments like: 'Are you ready yet?' It was funny, but now, after all the success I've had, they just seemed to decide: 'Well, I guess we'll just leave you alone.' "

I n his rookie year of 1997, Nomar put together a 30-game hitting streak, tying an AL record. He also set a major-league record for RBIs by a leadoff hitter and for homers by a rookie shortstop. He amassed 209 hits—most by a rookie since Johnny Pesky over 50 years earlier. He became the first unanimous choice for rookie of the year since Carlton Fisk in 1969. Jimy Williams was immediately impressed with the rookie. "The kid plays like he's been here before," he said. "I don't know when or who he's played with, but I swear he's been here."

O n May 11, 1999, Nomar hit two grand slams in a single game and added a two-run homer, driving in a total of 10 runs! His first grand salami came on his first at-bat in the first inning; his two-run drive in his second at-bat in the third. In his final at-bat, in the eighth, Nomar hit his second bases-loaded homer, becoming only the third Red Sox player ever to hit two in a single game (the others were Jim Tabor and Rudy York). He also became the first Sox player to knock in 10 runs in a game since Freddie Lynn accomplished the feat.

I n a backward sort of way, Nomar was named after his father. His name is his father's name spelled backward: Ramon.

N omar loves the chemistry that exists on the current edition of the Red Sox. "In my rookie year,

Jeff Frye and Jim Corsi had a mild disagreement in the clubhouse before a game with the Chicago White Sox. Nothing serious at all. So then the game starts, and we're ahead of the White Sox by a run, and they get a runner on second late in the game. The manager brings in Corsi in relief. He has to face Frank Thomas *and* Albert Belle, so he's trying to psych himself up and get himself ready. We have a mound conference with the manager and Frye and me. As we're talking, Frye picks up the resin bag. First base is open, so we decide to walk Frank and pitch to Albert. Corsi's trying to pump himself up. He says: 'All right! All right! And he looks at me and Jeff Frye and says: 'We've gotta roll this up guys! Jeff, give me the resin bag.' And Jeff says: 'Hell no', and throws the resin bag on the ground and walks away like he's really mad. Then Corsi looks at me and says: 'Nomar, you've gotta turn this play for me, right?' I just shrug and say: 'Look Jim, I'm just a rookie. I've gotta stick with my second baseman. You're on your own.'

We were laughing as we ran back to our positions, and Corsi just stared at us in disbelief. He didn't even have the resin bag in his hand because Jeff had thrown it away. He was left standing there like a lost puppy dog. I'm sure he was thinking: *I'm about to face Albert Belle in a crucial spot in a big game and my second baseman and shortstop have just told me to screw myself.* It was like a mutiny.

"He walks Frank Thomas as planned and then makes the first pitch to Belle. Albert hits the ball in the hole, and I come out of nowhere to backhand it and

Nomar Garciaparra

throw off-balance to Frye. Frye grabs it out of nowhere, wheels and throws to first, and we turn the most unbelievable double play you've ever seen. As we're running to the dugout, Corsi says: 'Yeah! Yeah! Thanks guys!' And we say: 'That wasn't for you. Screw you! We wanted to win in spite of you.' It was just the funniest thing. Jeff and I almost died laughing. We messed with him and then went out there and made an unbelievable play for him. We have a great bunch of guys; we really do. Everybody gets along well. It just makes it so much fun to come to the ballpark every day."

Somebody once asked Nomar what he thought of the curse of the Bambino. "I said: 'I'm from L.A., I don't know what the heck you're talking about.' Some things I guess it's just best I don't know. I just said: 'I play for the Red Sox NOW. We're going to start our own tradition here. And then you can talk about *us* in years to come.' "

If his first few years are any indication, Nomar probably can't wait for next season to begin. In his rookie year of 1997, he batted .306 with 30 homers and 98 RBI. In 1998, he hit .323 with 35 HR (only the fifth player in major league history to hit at least 30 HR in each of his first two years) and 122 RBI. In 1999, he finished with a .357 average, 27 home runs and 104 RBIs. If he hadn't missed 27 games due to injury, he would have exceeded 200 hits. He finished with 190. Individual statistics don't mean much to this young man, however. "Every year I have just one goal in mind, and that's to win the World Series. That's it. And if I ever win it, then I'll say: 'You know what? My other fingers are a little bit lonely.' "

As a rookie, Ted Williams once said that his goal was to be able to walk down the street after his career was over and be acknowledged as the greatest hitter of them all. Does Nomar have similar career goals? "When it's all done, I would just like to be able to walk down the street and have people say: 'There goes Nomar—a great player who's just like us. One of those guys who really loved the game.' "

Dick Gernert

In June 1953, the Detroit Tigers visited Fenway Park, and the carnage that ensued was of biblical proportions. On June 17, sparked by first baseman Dick Gernert's two home runs and four RBIs, the Red Sox tamed the tabbies 17-1. But this was just the color cartoon before the next day's main feature. On June 18, the Red Sox once again scored 17 runs, only this time they did it in a single seventh-inning barrage! A total of 23 Red Sox hitters came to the plate in the record-setting frame, and 20 of them reached base. Gernert once again led the charge with a home run and four RBIs. The Sox added 11 singles, two doubles and six walks in this pitcher's nightmare, including a bases-loaded walk to Gernert. Gene Stephens recorded three of the record 14 hits in the inning, which dragged on for 48 minutes. The final score of 23-3 was more suited to the NFL's Patriots and Lions. Asked about his memories of this extraordinary series, the modest Gernert replied: "I remember that the next game they beat us."

Billy Goodman

B illy Goodman was a good-hitting second baseman for the Red Sox from 1947 to 1957, leading the American League in 1950 with a .354 mark. While in the field, he had the habit of chewing on blades of grass between pitches. "He ate so much of the infield around second base, the ground had a curve in it," claims Mickey McDermott. "One time I asked him: 'What do you do in the wintertime, farm yourself out?' His teeth were like a leprechaun's."

In 1950, the year he captured the American League batting title, Billy Goodman had no regular fielding position and was called the "one-man bench." In the days before the DH, Billy Goodman couldn't readily break into the strong Sox infield. His third full season with the Red Sox was 1950. That year, the Red Sox had Walt Dropo at first. He led the league with 144 RBI in his rookie year. Bobby Doerr was, at that point, a veteran seven-time All-Star second baseman who hit .294 and led the league in triples that year, tied with Sox center fielder Dom DiMaggio. Vern Stephens played short and played in his sixth All-Star Game in 1950. Stephens hit .300. Not wanting to be overshadowed by the rookie Dropo, Stephens also knocked in 144 runs to tie for the league lead. Johnny Pesky held down the hot corner and sported a .312 average. The outfield didn't offer many openings either. The outfielders were Dom DiMaggio (.328), Al Zarilla (.325) and Ted Williams (a disappointing .317, after breaking his elbow in the All-Star Game.)

So what could Goodman do? A true utility player, he fit in where he could, when he could, and amassed 150 hits in 424 at-bats, for a league-leading .354. Not bad for a guy who didn't have a steady position.

Mike Greenwell

A fiery player who reportedly wrestled alligators in the off-season, Greenwell once irritated his teammates by calling them "a bunch of wimps and fairies." The man they called "Gator" even got into a fight with fellow Soxer Mo Vaughn behind the batting cage during batting practice. Most people would rather tackle the alligators. In 1996, he knocked in all nine runs in a Red Sox victory over Seattle.

Lefty Grove

U nlike the Yankees' easy going Lefty Gomez, Red Sox southpaw pitcher Lefty Grove was famous for his foul temper. Ted Williams suggested: "He was a tantrum thrower like me but smarter. When he punched a locker, he always did it with his right hand. He was a careful tantrum thrower."

W hen he threw punches at lockers, he threw them with his right hand so he wouldn't hurt his pitching arm. No matter how angry he was, he always protected that salary wing. Once, years later, he gave some free advice on the subject to Bill Werber, when the two were teammates on the Red Sox. Werber also possessed a fine temper, and one day he got so mad at himself that he kicked a full water bucket and broke his toe. "Never," advised Grove, "kick a full water bucket. Pick out an empty one. And never kick it with your toe. Kick it with your whole foot."

I t has been said of Red Sox Hall of Fame pitcher Lefty Grove: "He could throw a lamb chop past a hungry wolf." Grove led the American League in ERA nine times.

Carroll Hardy

C arroll Hardy is probably best known as the only player to ever pinch hit for the great Ted Williams, which is like asking Snoop Doggy Dogg to go on for Pavarotti. Williams had fouled a ball off his foot and been forced to leave the game. Actually, it was one of three notable pinch-hitting assignments by Hardy. While playing for the Cleveland Indians in 1958, he also pinch hit for future record-breaker Roger Maris— and proceeded to hit his first major-league homer. In 1961, he was called to pitch hit for a promising but temporarily struggling newcomer named Carl Yastrzemski. And when Ted Williams hit a home run in his last at-bat in baseball, and left the game to a thunderous ovation, it was Carroll Hardy who replaced him in left field.

Tommy Harper

S peedster Tommy Harper is the all-time single-season Red Sox stolen base king with 54 swipes in 1973. As he approached Tris Speaker's previous record of 52, the Red Sox announced that when he stole his 53rd, the game would be halted and the base presented to Harper. "In that case," said Harper mischievously, "I'm going to try stealing home. I want to stand there while they dig it up." The Red Sox were probably pleased that the record steal took place at second base instead.

Ken Harrelson

S porting Nehru jackets and love beads, Ken "Hawk" Harrelson was the Red Sox fashion plate and trendsetter in the late sixties. The Hawk, whose impressive nose resembled that noble bird's beak, reportedly had two hotel rooms, one for himself and one for his extensive wardrobe of mod clothes. Harrelson was also the first player to wear a batting glove, which was actually a converted golf glove.

Dave (Hendu) Henderson:

From Goat To Gloat

The Red Sox trailed the Angels 3 games to 1 in the 1986 American League Championship Series. The score was 5-4 in favor of the Angels with the Red Sox batting in the top of the ninth. With two out, reliever Gary Lucas was brought in to replace Angels starter Mike Witt. Lucas promptly hit Rich Gedman with a pitch. Angels manager Gene Mauch then brought in right-hander Donnie Moore to face Dave Henderson. With the count at 1-2, Hendu fouled off two pitches and then homered into the left field seats to give the Red Sox the lead and steal the game for the Red Sox. Henderson was wearing the goat's horns earlier in the contest as he had a ball go off his glove for a home run. Innings later, he won the ALCS game for the Red Sox with a dramatic HR.

Butch Hobson

Before becoming the Red Sox's gritty but erratic third baseman, Butch Hobson had been a triple option quarterback for Bear Bryant at the University of Alabama. The first quarterback to play on Astroturf in Tuscaloosa, his elbows took a beating from blindside tackles. "That's why he could throw around corners, but he could never throw straight to first base," explains Bill Lee.

Harry Hooper

Hooper is considered by many to be the greatest defensive right fielder who ever played the game. He was the first AL player to use flip-down sunglasses and also pioneered the sliding catch. No less an authority than the great Walter Johnson called him "the toughest out of all in a pinch." Hooper also stole 300 bases for the Sox.

Hooper was an integral part of the last Red Sox World Series champions of 1918, and he also contributed greatly to bringing the championship to Boston in 1912. In Game Eight (yes, Game Eight; Game Two was stopped on account of darkness) of the '12 Series, Hooper, with a little help from above, made one of the greatest catches in Series history.

With the score knotted at 1-1 in the ninth, Hooper was running to his position in right field. Seeing something on the ground, he knelt to pick it up and discovered that it was a small piece of paper with a picture of the Sacred Heart of Jesus and a prayer. "I read the prayer as I went out to my position," recalled Hooper years later. "Then I put the picture in my pocket."

New York Giant Larry Doyle laid into a pitch and drove it to the deepest part of right field. If it had fallen in, it would have given the Giants the lead and probably ended the game. Instead, the Divinely inspired Hooper made a sensational bare-handed catch to save a run and send the game into extra innings. The Sox went on to win the game in the bottom of the tenth. Hooper was quite willing to share the glory: "The way I caught the ball—how I was in the exact spot and position to catch it and how I caught it—was as if someone had placed it in my hand."

Ralph Houk

Ralph Houk, who would later go on to manage both the Yankees and Red Sox, was a rookie catcher for the New York Yankees in 1947. The Yankees were playing the Red Sox with fastball specialist Frank Shea on the mound for New York. With Ted Williams approaching the plate, Houk decided to try a new strategy. Knowing that Williams was a great fastball hitter and would be expecting the heater, Houk decided to try to fool him by calling for a change-up. Ted adjusted to the slower pitch and drove a blue-darter straight back through the box for a double, almost maiming Shea in the process. Later, in the Yankee dugout, manager Bucky Harris asked young Houk what the pitch had been. "It was change of pace," Houk sheepishly replied. "Well, he sure as hell changed the pace of it, didn't he?" said Harris dryly.

Jackie Jensen

One of Boston's best players, Jackie Jensen, had a fear of flying. In fact, it caused him to retire from the game on two separate occasions. While on terra firma, Jensen compiled some impressive figures, however. In 1958, he captured the MVP award in the American League by hitting 35 home runs and driving in 122.

In June 1961, Jackie Jensen's fear of flying caused him to refuse to fly to Detroit for a game the next day. Instead, he drove 850 miles and still managed to be in the lineup for the first pitch.

Jensen holds the rare distinction of having played in the Rose Bowl, the World Series and the All-Star Game.

Smead Jolley

The area in front of the 37' Green Monster in Fenway's left field once featured an incline known as Duffy's Cliff (named after Red Sox left fielder Duffy Lewis, who was particularly adept at playing there). One time, Red Sox manager Marty McManus spent hours trying to teach good-hit, no-field left fielder Smead Jolley to negotiate the treacherous piece of outfield. When Jolley tried to apply his newly acquired knowledge, he went up the incline smoothly, making a nice catch of the ball. Unfortunately, on the way back down he landed on his posterior, and the ball fell to the ground.

"For the love of God!" the frustrated McManus bellowed. "I spent all that time teaching you to climb up the cliff and then you screw it up."

Replied Jolley: "I guess you should have spent some time showing me how to come back down."

La Notizia was a newspaper devoted to Bostonians of Italian descent. In the mid-30s, well before the

Red Sox lineup featured any Conigliaros or Petrocellis, the paper's inventive sports editor converted Smead Jolley into a paisano by assigning him the humorous name of Smeederino Jolliani.

Jack Kramer

Jack Kramer was one of the most stylish players in Red Sox history. Known as "Handsome Jack," he reportedly changed clothes for breakfast, lunch and dinner. A finesse pitcher with little speed, fellow Red Sox pitcher Mickey McDermott claims: "When Kramer threw his fastball, three birds shit on it before it reached home plate."

The Red Sox have not always been one big happy family. Friction sometimes existed between players with different personalities and temperaments. Catcher Matt Batts and pitcher Jack Kramer were an example of this. As batteries go, they were negatively charged. Once, while Batts was warming Kramer up in front of a large Fenway Park crowd, he told teammate Mel Parnell to pay close attention. Batts then removed his glove and proceeded to catch Kramer's next offering with his bare hands—the ultimate insult to any pitcher. Kramer was incensed, refusing to have Batts warm him up ever again.

Bill Lee

B ill Lee will never make the Hall of Fame. Not unless some slightly warped visionary decides to open a wing for the flakes, free spirits and characters who have spiced up the grand old game over the years. If that unlikely event occurs, Lee will be first in line for admission to a ward that will also confine the likes of Moe Drabowsky, Mark Fidrych, Jay Johnstone, Mickey McDermott and Daffy Dean.

Lee was an above average pitcher—not Hall of Fame material but a solid major-league starter. Never a fire-baller, the crafty southpaw got by with a fine repertoire of curves and sliders, interspersed with a mediocre fastball. When the speed limit in Massachusetts was lowered, a Massachusetts TV ad advised drivers not to exceed Bill Lee's fastball—55 miles per hour.

Bill Lee was never a clown; never an Absorbine Junior-in-your jock jokester. Lee's brand of humor was slightly more cerebral. He was the thinking man's flake; a kind of lower class Yogi Berra with better diction. Lee was dubbed "the Spaceman" because in the conservative, buttoned-down world of baseball, he had an absolutely unique view of the baseball world. And he wasn't shy about sharing this perspective with anyone who'd listen. He once had his foot X-rayed and suggested to the doctor: "That loose thing's just an old Dewar's cap floating around." Lee was eventually traded from Boston to Montreal for Stan Papi, despite the fact that he was the third winningest left-hander in Red Sox history (after Mel Parnell and Lefty Grove.)

Lee and his manager Don Zimmer seldom saw eye to eye. The low point came when Lee labeled the puffy-cheeked Zimmer "the gerbil," a nickname adopted by some in the Boston media. "I was actually praising him when I called him a gerbil," argues Lee. "I had said that Yankees manager Billy Martin was a no-good dirty rat and Zimmer was not that way. He's given his life to baseball. His fatal flaw was that he was a manager in a city where, as a visiting player, he had a very difficult time with pitchers. Pitching is 90% of the game of baseball, and pitching happened to be the stuff that got him out 80% of the time. He was a .200 hitter, and that is what dictated the way he thought about pitchers."

The 1978 Red Sox blew a 14-game lead and ultimately lost a playoff game to the Yankees. When southpaw Bill Lee was subsequently traded from the Red Sox to the Expos at the end of the season, he was asked if he was upset to leave. His reply: "Who wants to be on a team that goes down in history with the '64 Phillies and the '67 Arabs?"

When his friend and soul mate Bernie Carbo was sold to the Cleveland Indians, Bill "Spaceman" Lee went on an unofficial strike—jumping the club and going home. He was finally tracked down by Red Sox president Haywood Sullivan, who informed Lee that he must dock him a day's pay, amounting to about $500. Lee's reply? "Make it fifteen hundred. I'd like to have the whole weekend."

Before the anticlimactic seventh game of the 1975 World Series, Cincinnati Reds manager Sparky Anderson boasted that no matter what the outcome of the game, his starting pitcher Don Gullett was going to the Hall of Fame. Bill Lee, the Red Sox starter, countered with: "No matter what the outcome of the game, I'm going to the Eliot Lounge." And he did.

Lee once charged that the California Angels "could hold batting practice in the lobby of the Grand Hotel (in Anaheim) and not chip a chandelier."

The World According to Chairman Lee:

" *That's like having a Mercedes and hanging little dice from the rearview mirror.* "–Bill Lee, on the Red Sox installing a new electronic scoreboard in Fenway Park.

" *My first edict if I were Commissioner of Baseball would be to get rid of the designated hitter, to bring back the 25-man roster, to get rid of Astroturf, maintain smaller ballparks and revamp quality old ballparks. I'd outlaw video instant replays. I'd outlaw mascots. I'd put organic foods in the stands. I would make cold, pasteurized beer mandatory from small breweries located near the ballparks—no giant multi-national breweries. I would bring back warm, roasted peanuts. Just the smell of grass and those warm, roasted peanuts should be enough to make people come to the park. I would just try to reduce it to an organic game; the way it used to be.* "–Bill Lee

" *My policy would be no guns; no butter. They'll both kill you. Tear down the defenses. Ted Williams will be my Secretary of Defense. He'll go out and tear down all defenses just like he did the Boudreau shift.* "–Bill Lee, on what he'd do if he were President of the United States.

Bill Lee

B ill Lee on Carl Yastrzemski: *"He's a dull, boring potato farmer from Long Island who just happened to be a great ballplayer. But he was the worst dresser in organized baseball. He made Inspector Columbo look like a candidate for Mr. Blackwell's list of best-dressed men. He had the same London Fog raincoat during his entire*

career. We'd throw it in trashcans all around the league, and somehow it mysteriously made its way back."

B ill Lee on pre-game habits: *"I told (reporters) that I sprinkled marijuana on my organic buckwheat pancakes, and then when I ran my five miles to the ballpark, it made me impervious to the bus fumes. That's when (Baseball Commissioner) Bowie Kuhn took me off his Christmas list."*

A fter the Red Sox lost Game Two of the 1975 World Series to even the Series at 1-1 with the Cincinnati Reds, starting pitcher Bill Lee was asked: "Bill, how would you characterize the World Series so far?" Reporters waited for fresh insights from the Red Sox Zen philosopher. His reply: "Tied."

W hen umpire Larry Barnett failed to make an interference call on hitter Ed Armbrister at home plate in a much-publicized incident that may have cost the Red Sox the '75 World Series, Bill Lee felt that Sox manager Darrell Johnson had not argued the call with sufficient vigor. "I'd have bitten Barnett's ear off," said Lee. "I'd have van Goghed him!"

Jim Lonborg

J im Lonborg was one of the most stylish right-handed pitchers in Red Sox history. Gentleman Jim was best known for his league-leading 22 wins during the Red Sox 1967 drive to the American League pennant. He is also famous for his courageous effort in a losing cause in Game Seven of that year's World Series. Lonborg was pitching on just two days' rest. After the game, he was surrounded by reporters, curious about the mental strain of such an ordeal. "It has to be physical," insisted Lonborg. "That's why I'm soaking my arm now. If it was mental, I'd be soaking my head."

E ven in the midst of the pressure packed '67 pennant drive, the Red Sox maintained their sense of humor. Nothing and no one was sacred. Carl Yastrzemski used to annoy his pitchers by not even turning around to pursue sure home runs to left field. The Red Sox mound fraternity thought that to save them embarrassment, he should at least pretend that these long homers might be catchable. When Cleveland's Max Alvis hit a shot over the Green Monster off ace Jim Lonborg, Yaz didn't move a muscle. Back in the dugout at the end of the half inning, Lonborg cornered him. "You could at least make it look like you might possibly catch it," he suggested. Yastrzemski was unrepentant. "I might have if they moved the stadium back a hundred yards or so," he said.

Sparky Lyle

Aside from being one of the best relief pitchers in major-league history, Sparky Lyle was famous for dropping his pants and sitting on birthday cakes. According to Bill Lee, that's what prompted one of the worst trades in Red Sox history. "He sat on (Red Sox owner) Tom Yawkey's cake, and Yawkey found out," claims Lee. "The next day Lyle is shipped off to the Yankees and here comes Danny Cater. All because of sitting on a birthday cake."

Fred Lynn

When former Red Sox center fielder Fred Lynn first came up to the big leagues in 1975, he was platooned against southpaw pitchers. The first game he ever played in Milwaukee, the left-handed batter hit a home run his first time up, a double the next time up

Fred Lynn

and then was removed for a pinch hitter the next time up against a left-handed reliever. Recalls Lynn: "I thought to myself: *This is some tough league!*"

In 1975, Fred Lynn became the first and only player to win both the Rookie of the Year and the MVP in the same year. On June 18 that year, he tied an American League record by hitting for 16 total bases. Lynn also set the new record for doubles by a rookie with 47.

Steve Lyons

When erratic, off-the-wall Steve Lyons was traded to the Chicago White Sox for soon-to-be Hall of Famer Tom Seaver, a Baltimore reporter dubbed the trade: "Cy Young for Psy-cho!" The *Boston Globe* headline proclaiming the trade was as follows: SEAVER FINALLY CHANGES HIS SOX. Lyons actually had four separate stints with the Red Sox.

Steve Lyons and teammate Marty Barrett once both slid into second base—from opposite directions—

on a ball hit to the outfield. The center fielder was so startled he overthrew the ball into the dugout, allowing both runners to score.

Frank Malzone

L eo Durocher was once asked if Red Sox third baseman Frank Malzone had any faults. "Dandruff maybe," replied the veteran manager.

Pedro Martinez

W hen Roger Clemens left Boston for Toronto, the Red Sox brought in right-handed pitcher Pedro Martinez, nine years his junior, from the Montreal Expos. Pedro promptly created his own legend in Beantown. Arriving amid the hoopla of a six-year, $75 million contract, the 5'11", 170-pound native of the Dominican Republic was immediately worshipped by the Fenway Faithful. What did the new millionaire do with his newfound wealth? A luxury car perhaps, or a mansion in the suburbs? Why, he built a church of course—The Immaculate Conception in his home village of Manoguayabo. "That was better than a Cy Young to me," said Martinez.

I n the summer of 1999, Pedro Martinez achieved god-like status in New England. His appeal crossed all ethnic and religious lines. Late in the season, with Pedro leading American League pitchers in virtually every statistical category, the following story appeared in the *Boston Herald:* apparently a Jewish Red Sox fan went to his rabbi before Rosh Hashanah and said, "Rabbi, I have a problem. I know it's Rosh Hashanah, but it's Yankees-Red Sox and Pedro is pitching." The Rabbi replied thoughtfully: "It's not such a problem. It's for nights like this that God invented VCRs." Sox fan: "So, I can tape the Rosh Hashanah services?"

E ven his teammates become wide-eyed fans when Pedro is weaving his mound magic. "When Pedro is pitching and striking out all those guys, it's amazing to watch," says shortstop Nomar Garciaparra. "Last summer (1999), he struck out 16 Atlanta Braves in an inter-league contest at Fenway. The trouble is you end up watching him and you become a fan as you're watching him. I remember everyone is cheering every strikeout he's making, and they're going crazy. It was kind of funny because if we made a play, they were kind of mad at us.

They wanted to see him strike out everybody. I remember we were winning, and the last hitter of the game hits a ball between short and third, and I didn't even move! And I think it took [John] Valentin a little bit of time to move—because we were almost hypnotized. But this play was so funny because the guy hit it, and all the fans went: "Awww . . . he didn't strike him out." All the fans were upset—and I was the same way, going "Awww . . . too bad." Then all of a sudden I realized: "Oh shit, I've got to go and make a play." It was a good thing Valentin got it because I was nowhere to be found. He made the play for the final out and the game was over, but it was really strange. That's the way he was—amazing. You become mesmerized. "

I n capturing the 1999 Cy Young Award, Martinez put together what many consider—in relative terms— the best pitching performance in the history of baseball. At the age of 28, Pedro dominated American League hitters like no other pitcher before or since. He won 23 games, lost only four and compiled a 2.07 ERA, more than one full run ahead of any other pitcher. He struck out 313 (over 100 more than the next best) and allowed only 37 bases on balls.

While on the mound, Pedro is dead serious, but in the dugout he is a different man. He has been known to patrol the dugout in a Yoda mask, and he directs a continuous stream of chatter toward opposing players and teammates. He has even coined a few original baseball terms. According to the Martinez dictionary, a "dog fart" is a bloop single, a "ding-dong johnson" is a homer, and an "underwater johnson" is a slow swing.

When the Chicago White Sox took issue with some of his dugout dialogue during the 1999 season, teammates Nomar Garciaparra, Damon Buford, Mark Portugal and Bret Saberhagen devised a plot to keep their ace under control. "Pedro Martinez likes to talk a lot when he's not playing," confirms teammate Nomar Garciaparra. "He gets very animated out there in the dugout. It's good . . . but at times it's like: *All right already, Pedro! That's enough!* One day we were beating the Chicago White Sox pretty good, and he was talking to the White Sox players and messing with them. I was sitting there watching as he was leaning up against the dugout post, and I said to the guys: 'You know what? Why don't we just tape him to this post? Maybe that'll calm him down, and then at least he can't walk around all over the place. It'll keep him quiet.' So we just started taping and taping. We were going to keep it going. At first, he was unconcerned. Then as we kept taping, he started realizing that he really couldn't move. We didn't care; we just kept going. He was still talking, and I said; 'We've forgotten

Pedro Martinez

one very big thing. We've got to tape his mouth up, too.' And then we taped up his mouth. Finally the game was over, and we just ran out and left him there.

"The White Sox were really good sports about it. He wanted to come out and shake hands, but he couldn't. He was stuck there. The only reason we didn't leave him tied up was that he was scheduled to pitch the next day. Otherwise, I'll tell you what—you would have seen him in the same uniform in the same spot when they sang the National Anthem the next afternoon."

" *Pedro's a funny guy. He really enjoys the game, but on days when he's pitching—as soon as the game starts—it's all business."* – Nomar Garciaparra

It was billed as the Duel of the Century; the Gunfight at the OK Corral. Instead, when Pedro Martinez faced Roger Clemens in Game Three of the 1999 American League Championship Series, it turned out to be Cy Young vs. Cy Old; Don Larsen vs. Dawn of Time. Pedro was masterful, striking out a Red Sox-record 12 Yankees (including Derek Jeter and Paul O'Neill twice) en route to a 13-1 thrashing of the hated Yanks. It was baseball's dominant team vs. baseball's dominant player as Martinez handed the Yankees their only loss in 19 postseason encounters. Pedro allowed only two hits and no runs before being removed after seven innings of work. Many Red Sox fans took this victory as retribution against the traitorous Clemens, who had departed Boston for more money a few years earlier. What made the win especially sweet for Martinez is the fact that he had only one of his usual tools working for him on the mound. Hobbled with a strained muscle in his back, Martinez should not have been on the mound at all. His fastball, usually clocked in the 96-98 range, was well under 90; his change-up was mediocre; his curveball lacked its usual sharpness. Only his amazing pitching intellect allowed him to bamboozle Yankee hitters for seven innings and inflict the worst defeat the Bronx Bombers had absorbed in their proud history of post-season play.

When Pedro won the 1997 Cy Young Award, he presented it to his fellow Dominican and idol, Hall of Fame pitcher Juan Marichal.

Mickey McDermott

When fuzzy-cheeked teenager Mickey McDermott first came up to the Red Sox, the management tried to protect the young man from the temptations of the road. One day, he was called into manager Joe Cronin's office. Cronin explained that McDermott had been seen in a nightclub drinking with veteran pitcher Ellis Kinder, also known as "Old Folks." "You cannot be seen with Kinder in nightclubs!" lectured Cronin. "You've got your whole future ahead of you." McDermott denied that he had been at a nightclub the previous evening. Cronin told him to go look in the mirror. When he did, he saw that his tongue was completely green from drinking grasshoppers. "You look like a %$#&ing leprechaun," said Cronin.

Aside from being an above-average pitcher, McDermott was also a talented singer. Once, he pitched 16 innings against Cleveland, but in the 16th he faltered, loading the bases. Birdie Tebbetts, who had just been traded from the Red Sox to the Indians shouted from the dugout: "Sing your $%#*ing way out of this, McDermott!"

The Red Sox sent McDermott to live with Johnny Pesky, hoping that the stability of family life would have a calming effect on the young pitcher. It didn't work. "They gave him a car one time as a tribute on Pesky Day," recalls Mickey. "I borrowed it that night and I got some broad, and I kicked the window out trying to get laid in the back seat. He was going to kill me. I said 'Why didn't you have it open? I'm 6'3"; you're only 5'11".' "

McDermott thinks that he deserves to have his name associated with a Fenway landmark, just as Johnny Pesky does on the right field foul pole known as Pesky's Pole. "What about putting my %$#& name on the Wall? Batters hit the *&^%ing Wall ninety million times thanks to me. I threw it, they hit it, and I ain't got my name on it or nothin'. I didn't even get a trophy, and Pesky got a freakin' pole named after him! I put Joe DiMaggio in the Hall of Fame. I threw it, and he hit it. I went to Joe one time and said: 'You owe me fifty thousand dollars.' 'For what?' he said. I said: 'You son of a bitch, I put you in the Hall of Fame.' So he autographed a ball to me saying: 'To Maurice, thank you for all the nice fastballs at Fenway Park.' Because of me, he killed three people on the Charles River rowing a boat."

Mickey McDermott: *"I once pinch-hit in Chicago, and on the mound was Virgil Trucks. Ted Williams could hit Trucks after midnight so he said: 'C'mere, bush. Listen, look for his slider.' I walked to the plate, and Trucks threw three fastballs right down the middle of the plate and struck me out. I walked back to the dugout and I said: 'Listen, Theodore, let me tell you a little story: my*

Mickey McDermott

name is NOT Ted Williams.' He said: 'You know, bush, you're finally getting smart.' "

B oston's ace left-hander Mel Parnell was McDermott's roommate on the Red Sox. Parnell once confided to manager Joe McCarthy: "We'd been on the road for a year, and I haven't seen him yet. I'm rooming with his suitcases."

A fter six years in Boston and two with the lowly Washington Senators, McDermott was traded in 1956 to the New York Yankees where he played under the legendary Casey Stengel. On a road trip to Boston, McDermott was quick to return to his old watering holes. Returning to the Kenmore Hotel at four in the morning, McDermott thought that he could use his intimate knowledge of Boston hotels to sneak past his ever-vigilant manager. More than a little inebriated, he sneaked into the basement of the hotel and used the service elevator to reach his floor. Unfortunately, McDermott forgot that Stengel had played and man-aged in Boston and also knew the city like the back of his hand. When the elevator door opened, there stood Stengel. The two faced each other eyeball to eyeball. Finally Stengel said in disgust: "Drunk again!" Stagger-ing past him down the hallway, McDermott hiccuped loudly and replied: "Me too, Skip!" Stengel was so amused he allowed the infraction to go unpunished.

McDermott was like a son to manager Joe McCarthy. Proud Irishmen both, the wayward pitcher and stern disciplinarian established an immediate rapport. One day, McCarthy called the 18-year-old McDermott into his office. "Maurice, do you have a girlfriend?" he asked. "Yes, sir," replied the young southpaw. "Did you ever hear of Lefty Gomez?" the manager continued. Again McDermott replied in the affirmative. "Well," said McCarthy, "don't become Lefty Gomez! He left his fastball in the sheets." McDermott was puzzled. "I was only 18; I didn't know what he was talking about. I wondered what the hell he'd leave his fastball in my sheets for. I was looking for it for three days."

A few years ago, McDermott was visiting the Ted Williams Museum in Hernando, Florida, for the annual Hitters' Hall of Fame induction ceremony. The Splendid Splinter was entertaining his good friends and honored guests President George Bush and wife Barbara. As McDermott was walking past the rostrum, Ted called out: "Maurice, come on over here." He then proceeded to introduce him to the President. "Well for chrissake, George, how the hell are you?" said McDermott. Embarrassed, Ted stammered: "I can't believe you addressed the President of the United States as George." McDermott replied: "Wait a minute, Theodore. He played against my friend Walt Dropo when he was at Yale and Walt was at Connecticut. Right, George?" Laughing at Williams' discomfort, Bush gave McDermott a high five.

McDermott sees some interesting parallels between baseball and marriage. "All my wives became umpires. They all said: 'Out!' "

According to the authors of *The Great American Baseball Card Flipping, Trading and Bubble Gum Book,* McDermott is: "the only player in the history of the Poughkeepsie, New York, public school system to be chosen unanimously by his high school graduating class as the man most likely to be found dead in his hotel room."

Sam Mele

While in Boston, Sam Mele played under legendary disciplinarian Joe McCarthy, who would not abide alibis or excuses of any kind. One bright, sunny day in 1949, Mele was playing Fenway's right field, an infamous 'sun field,' when a line drive was hit in his direction. The ball took a bad bounce, and Sam ducked as the ball caromed over his head. As he came to the dugout at the end of the inning, Mele made his second and more costly error—this one with McCarthy. "Oh geez, the ball got lost in the sun, and I didn't have time to pull my sunglasses down," he whined. "You know something, my boy?" replied Marse Joe. "They play all night games in Washington." Mele finished out the year where the sun never shone—with the lowly Senators in the basement of the American League.

Lou Merloni

The names have been omitted to protect the guilty, but the Red Sox's Lou ("The Igloo?") Merloni reports that while certain teammates were busy on the field, an unnamed Red Sox player used to put their sneakers in a freezer in a pan of water. After the game, while that player was in the shower, the frozen sneakers were placed in front of the player's locker, resulting in Red Sox and blue feet. The same cold-blooded perpetrator would also take players' clothes, roll them up, wet them and then freeze them before returning them to the players' lockers.

Merloni's best buddy on the Red Sox is Nomar Garciaparra, and while Lou has yet to achieve the level of success enjoyed by the young shortstop, they both share a great enthusiasm for the game. "Lou is an unbelievable player," says Nomar. "An absolute riot and a great person in the dugout. The kind of person every team needs. The best comment I heard—and it's so true—is what Jimy Williams said about him. He said: 'Your friend over there plays like he's trying to get to another level. He doesn't realize that this is as high as you can get.'"

Ed Morris

Red Sox pitcher Ed Morris (42-45 lifetime; 419 ERA) was stabbed to death at his own farewell party as he prepared to leave for spring training in 1932.

Trot Nixon

Humiliating rookies is a practice as old and honored as the game of baseball itself. On Sunday, September 19, 1999, the Red Sox, in the midst of an AL East pennant race with the hated Yankees, were hosting the Detroit Tigers at Fenway. In the top of the eighth, with the Red Sox up 7-3, the near-capacity Fenway crowd broke into spontaneous applause. Savvy fans knew what was up. Glancing toward the out-of-town scoreboard they saw that the Yankees were losing to Cleveland 7-6—and in a pennant race, that's more than enough to get a Boston crowd excited. Newcomers to Fenway, however, might be a bit confused—even those in uniform.

Red Sox right fielder Trot Nixon, a promising rookie who had homered in his previous at-bat, had no idea what was going on. As the applause grew in intensity, veteran center fielder Damon Buford explained that the fans were paying tribute to him for the home run he'd hit and that it was traditional to acknowledge such a tribute with a tip of the hat. Not wanting to appear ungrateful, Nixon reluctantly obliged. Not until the end of the inning did he realize that he had been had. "What happened to the camaraderie?" the embarrassed freshman moaned to reporters. "Love in the outfield? There's no love there! Next time I won't even listen to him."

Troy O'Leary

In Games Four and Five of the 1999 Cleveland-Boston series, first John Valentin and then Troy O'Leary drove in seven runs in back-to-back games. In O'Leary's case, he taught Indians manager Mike Hargrove a little bit about respect in the process. Because red-hot Nomar Garciaparra had homered in the first inning, Hargrove elected to walk Nomar in the third, despite the fact that the strategic ploy loaded the bases. O'Leary promptly hit the first offering out for a grand slam home run. In the seventh, Hargrove again decided to walk Nomar to pitch to Troy. Similar result—a three-run homer to win the game for the Red Sox. A few days later, Hargrove was out of a job. R-E-S-P-E-C-T! Sox it to me!

Johnny Orlando

When longtime Red Sox clubhouse man Johnny Orlando died, it was widely rumored that his friend Ted Williams scattered his ashes over the left field grass at Fenway Park. Supposedly, Orlando's will stipulated that his remains be spread on the ground where Williams had played. Authorities at Fenway Park apparently objected, and so Williams discreetly went out and carried out his friend's wish.

Mel Parnell

Mel Parnell was a left-handed Red Sox pitcher (1947-1956) and two-time 20-game winner. In 1953, he shut out the Yankees four times, and on July 14, 1956, at the age of 34, he pitched a no-hitter—a 4-0 shutout of the Chicago White Sox, the first for the Red Sox since 1923. The 1956 gem was the only no-hitter that a pitcher ended with an unassisted put-out. On the last play, the ball was hit back to Parnell on the first base side of the mound. He came off the mound and made the play and continued on to first base to record the final out. Red Sox first baseman Mickey Vernon said: "What's the matter, fella, you don't have any confidence in me?" Replied Parnell: "Mickey, I have all the confidence in the world in you. I just didn't have any in myself —I may have thrown it away."

The 1948 playoff-game loss to Cleveland is among the most disappointing games in Red Sox history. No one was more disappointed than southpaw ace Mel Parnell, who was expecting to start the game. Just before game time, manager Joe McCarthy told Parnell he had decided to go with right-hander Denny Galehouse instead. When the manager informed Galehouse of the change, Parnell says that the surprised pitcher "turned ghostly white." The Indians defeated the Sox 8-3 to capture the American League pennant.

Mel Parnell

Johnny Pesky

To many fans across New England, Johnny Pesky is Mr. Red Sox. In Game Seven of the 1946 World Series, Pesky was unfairly accused of holding the ball too long, allowing the St. Louis Cardinals' Enos Slaughter to dash home with the winning run. During the off-season, Pesky returned to his home state of Oregon to escape the unwanted attention from Boston fans and media. As part of his "therapy," he attended a college football game between Oregon and Oregon State. The two teams fumbled the ball throughout the sloppily played game, and the crowd became somewhat loud and abusive. Enjoying his anonymity, Pesky felt relaxed . . . until he heard a fan shout: "Give the ball to Pesky; he'll hold on to it."

Mel Parnell claims that he was responsible for naming Fenway's right-field foul pole "Pesky's Pole." "Johnny didn't have great power, but he had great bat control and could spray the ball around," says Parnell. "This made him a great number-two hitter hitting behind DiMaggio because if Dom got on, Johnny could move him around, either by bunting or by placing the ball. But every once in awhile he'd hit one out, curving it around that pole. I said: 'Johnny, that's your pole. That's Pesky's pole.' And it stuck."

Johnny Pesky achieved 11 straight hits in 1946—one short of the record held by two other Sox, Pinky Higgins and Dropo—and didn't realize it. When he came up the 12th time in a close game with George Metkovich on first base, Pesky decided to lay down a hit-and-run to protect him and move him over. The next two times up, Pesky got hits each time. Managers Joe Cronin and Joe McCarthy both gave Pesky the chance to call his own plays.

Pesky is one of two players who were in uniform for the only two American League sudden-death play-off games—in 1948 and 1978. Pesky played third base for the Red Sox in their 1948 loss to the Cleveland Indians and occupied the first-base coaching box in the 1978 loss to the Yankees. The man on the winning side on both occasions was Bob Lemon, who was a pitcher with the Indians in '48 and manager of the Yanks in '78.

On the last day of the season, Yaz sneaked into the clubhouse and cut up coach Johnny Pesky's clothes. Pesky had to fly back to Boston from Detroit wearing his uniform. Johnny got him back good, though, and quickly. Yaz caught a plane later that day and headed back to his home in Florida. His luggage, however, accompanied the team back to Boston. Johnny was waiting and grabbed Yaz's bag as the luggage was unloaded. He opened the bag and began passing out Yaz's clothes to passersby, shouting: "Here's a Yaz souvenir!" People began grabbing them and soon they were all gone. When Yaz eventually opened his suitcases, they were empty. In the mail some days later he found a Polaroid shot of Pesky with the clothes. Confronting Johnny with photographic evidence of his largesse, Johnny told Yaz: "I'm trying to take them back from the people."

Rico Petrocelli

Rico Petrocelli is one third of the answer to a great trivia question: There are three American League players—all former Red Sox—with ten or more letters in their names who have hit 40 or more homers in a season. Can you name them? (Answer: Tony Conigliaro, Carl Yastrzemski, Rico Petrocelli)

Rico Petrocelli

Jimmy Piersall

Jimmy Piersall arrived in Boston in 1952 with the reputation as a great fielder with some eccentricities. Teammate Mel Parnell recalls: "I remember pitching a game in Chicago, and I could hear a roar from right field. I turned to look, and all I could see was the number on Jimmy's back. He was facing the stand, leading a locomotive cheer of P-I-E-R-S-A-L-L. If the ball had been hit to right field, he would never have been able to make a play on it."

When former Red Sox center fielder Jimmy Piersall hit the 100th home run of his career while with the Mets, he celebrated by running around the bases backward—perfectly legal at that time but totally unorthodox.

The Red Sox sent Piersall to Birmingham, and apparently his reputation for erratic behavior preceded him. Teammate Mickey McDermott recalls one particular incident: "The umpire called him out on a bad pitch, and he didn't holler, he didn't say nothin', he just reached in his back pocket and pulled out a water pistol and shot the umpire with it. The umpire fainted dead away. After all the stories he'd read about Piersall, he said later: 'I thought the sonofabitch was going to kill me.' "

After his hospital treatment at Westborough State Hospital for mental illness, chronicled in his book *Fear Strikes Out,* Piersall couldn't recall anything from

Jimmy Piersall

over a year of his life. During that time, he played extremely well but was involved in fracas after fracas—fistfights, arguments and all sorts of shenanigans. He had to read news clippings about them later, much to his own mortification. He played to the crowd, taking melodramatic bows in center field after routine plays. He did calisthenics in the field. He ran in from his position behind Dom DiMaggio, imitating the Little Professor's distinctive trot on the way back to the dugout. He waved his arms like a chicken when Satchel Paige was pitching. He made oinking pig sounds. He agitated Paige so much that he lost his concentration and wound up surrendering a grand slam to Sammy White. White, for his part, joined in the clowning and crawled the last 10 feet to the plate, kissing it to make contact as the Sox won 11-9.

It was a cold and rainy April day at Fenway Park, and the game was delayed several times for pitching changes and sporadic downpours. During one such halt in proceedings, Piersall collected various debris thrown from the bleachers—popcorn containers, programs, newspapers and the like—and piled them behind the old center field flagpole. He then set them ablaze and warmed himself by the fire.

Dick Radatz

Dick "The Monster" Radatz stood 6'6" and tipped the scales at 240 pounds. The relief specialist was that rarest and most beloved phenomenon in Boston—a Yankee killer. Many Red Sox fans have an enduring image of Dick Radatz, arms raised straight up in a victory salute, walking off the mound after saving another game against the hated Yankees. He was also very cocky. In 1963, Red Sox pitcher Earl Wilson was leading the Yanks 2-1 in the ninth, but proceeded to load the bases. After a brief mound conference, Wilson let manager Johnny Pesky know that it might be time to bring on the Monster. Pesky brought in the fire-balling reliever to kill the New York rally. As the two pitchers met briefly at the mound, Radatz said to Wilson: "Why don't you crack me a beer? I'll be right in." Ten pitches and three strikeouts later, Mickey Mantle, Roger Maris and Elston Howard had been retired on strikes and Radatz was sharing a cool one with his appreciative teammate.

Jim Rice

Jim Rice was the Red Sox's best right-handed hitter since Jimmie Foxx and, also like Foxx, one of the strongest men in the major leagues. On more than one occasion he checked his swing and snapped the bat in half. Asked how he would position his outfield against Rice, Kansas City manager Whitey Herzog once said: "What I'd really like to do is put two guys on top of the CITGO sign and two in the net."

The number 406 holds double significance for Red Sox fans. Any fan worth his salt knows that in 1941 Ted Williams hit .406 to become the last man in major-league history to bat .400 for an entire season. But Jim Rice also achieved a 406 milestone. In 1978, the Red Sox strongman accumulated 406 total bases, the first to reach the 400 level since Hank Aaron managed exactly 400 in 1959. Rice became the first Ameri-

Jim Rice

can Leaguer to hit this elusive mark since Joe DiMaggio did it 41 years earlier. Rice had 213 hits, including 46 homers and 15 triples, and led the majors in both categories. He also led in RBIs (139) and slugging percentage (.600) while batting .315. He was named AL MVP.

Rice was the first player ever to amass over 200 hits and 35 home runs in three consecutive seasons ('77-'79.)

There was no wasted motion in Rice's powerful swing. One of strongest men ever to play the game, he boasted that he never lifted a weight. "Anyone who has to doesn't have a chance," he said. When that strength was uncorked with his short stride and flick of his bat, the results were often explosive. Rice loved his golf as well and had equal power in his drives. U.S. Open champion Lou Graham once said that Rice could hit a golf ball farther than anyone on the pro tour at the time.

Red Ruffing

Red Ruffing won 39 games and lost 96 (including 25 in 1928 alone) for the Red Sox—and still made it into the Hall of Fame! It was his good fortune to be traded to the Yankees, where he then won 231 while losing only 125. As a Red Sox pitcher, Ruffing had been 1 and 14 against the Yankees, but playing well in New York always seems to help in Hall of Fame voting. Ruffing had lost four toes on one foot in a coal mining accident and had to wear a special shoe. It was off Ruffing that Ted Williams hit the ball to the famous "red seat" at Fenway, more than halfway up the right-field bleachers.

Babe Ruth

When Babe Ruth first came up to the Red Sox it was as a pitcher, but even then he liked to hit. He insisted on taking his cuts in batting practice. One day, he arrived at the ballpark to discover that all his bats had been sawed in half by resentful teammates. Despite this setback, Ruth went on to have a rather respectable hitting career.

When Ruth was sold to the Yankees and moved from the pitcher's mound to the outfield, his former Red Sox teammate Tris Speaker offered the following words of wisdom: "Ruth made a grave mistake when he gave up pitching. Working once a week, he might have lasted a long time and become a great star."

On July 16, 1918, the Boston Red Sox and the St. Louis Browns were tied 1-1 in the bottom of the ninth. With a runner on first, Babe Ruth hit the ball out of the park to win the game. However, in those days, the game was declared over when the winning run scored, therefore Ruth was credited with a triple and not a home run.

After Red Sox owner Harry Frazee had sold Babe Ruth to the New York Yankees in order to finance a Broadway production of *No, No, Nanette,* Bostonians were justifiably outraged. One frigid January evening, Frazee and some friends from the theatrical world were out on the town. Frazee wanted to show that he was a man of some importance in the city. So, dressed in his best tuxedo, he hailed a cab and instructed the driver to proceed to Fenway Park. The cabbie overheard part of the backseat conversation and deduced who his passenger was. When they arrived at the ballpark, the driver asked: "Do you own the Red Sox?" Frazee replied proudly: "Why yes, my boy. Yes, I do." The cabbie promptly knocked Frazee on his ample posterior, shook his fist at him and said, "Then you're the %$&% who sold Babe Ruth to the Yankees." With that he drove off with the other passengers, leaving the dazed and bewildered owner sitting in a snow bank.

Babe Ruth

Ray Scarborough

Not many ballplayers win an argument with an umpire, but Red Sox pitcher Ray Scarborough did. Obtained from the Washington Senators, Scarborough brought with him a well-deserved reputation as the best bench jockey in baseball. He could get on guys and really run them ragged. At that time, Bill McGowan was considered the number-one umpire in the American League—at least by himself. One day, while umpiring behind home plate, he had missed several close pitches.

From the Sox dugout, Scarborough kept up a constant stream of verbal abuse. Finally, McGowan came over to the dugout and had a few choice words for his tormentor. Scarborough responded with a few choice words of his own. Things got so heated that McGowan ended up throwing his balls and strikes indicator at the mouthy pitcher. The indicator went under the players' bench, and Scarborough went down on all fours to retrieve it. When he finally found it, McGowan demanded that it be returned to him immediately. "Like hell," said Scarborough. "You can get it back from the league president." McGowan received a two-week suspension from the American League.

George Scott

Red Sox first baseman George "Boomer" Scott introduced a new name into the already-rich baseball lexicon. He called home runs "taters." It quickly caught on and was adopted by the likes of Reggie Jackson and other notables.

Scott used to wear a strange necklace strung with irregular shaped white objects. When a curious teammate asked what the objects were, the menacing Boomer replied: "The teeth of American League pitchers."

Bill Lee on George Scott: "I remember George Scott was in taking a shower, and Eddie Kasko was in taking a shower at the same time. George was lathering himself up with Head & Shoulders shampoo, and he had a big froth of it on his hair. Kasko, who was completely bald, looked over at George and said: 'Boy, I used to use that product quite a bit too!' Scott wasn't long rinsing his hair out."

When the Red Sox sent Sparky Lyle to the Yankees for Danny Cater, many fans felt it was the worst trade in Red Sox history. Cater was at bat in spring training, and a pitcher knocked him down—hit him in the bill of his cap and sent him spinning into the dust. Lying there, writhing around in real or imagined pain, he cried: "I can't see, I can't see!" Boomer Scott leaned over him and suggested: "Well, open up your eyes!"

George Scott

When Scott was traded to the Milwaukee Brewers, he almost won the Triple Crown. When he was traded back to Boston in 1977, however, he had lost much of his bat speed. Throwing batting practice for the Red Sox, coach Harvey Haddix threw out a challenge. "Boomer," he said, "I can throw nine fastballs in a row by you—up and in." Scott smirked: "Yeah, sure." Haddix, who was approaching sixty at the time, threw seven in a row past him before Scott finally fouled one off. Boomer said triumphantly: "See, I told you you couldn't do it!"

Eddie Shore

On June 23, 1917, Red Sox relief pitcher Eddie Shore tossed a perfect game against the Washington Senators. This is amazing enough on its own merit, but consider this: Shore wasn't the starting pitcher for the game; Babe Ruth was. After walking leadoff man Ed Foster, Ruth became involved in a heated dispute with the umpire and was ejected. Advising manager Jake Stahl that he "had nothing" that day, Shore nevertheless warmed up quickly and entered the game in relief of Ruth. Right away, Foster was gunned down at second in a steal attempt. Shore was flawless for the next

8 ²/₃ innings and was officially credited with a perfect game because he was on the mound for all 27 outs.

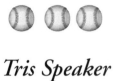

Tris Speaker

Tris Speaker was one of the greatest center fielders in baseball history. Outfield defense was the forte of "The Grey Eagle," who recorded 35 assists in 1912. In 1915, a slim (6'2,", 198 lbs.) young Red Sox pitcher named Babe Ruth dubbed Speaker "a fifth infielder" because he played incredibly shallow at his position. The grateful Babe had witnessed Speaker throw out runners at first on more than one occasion. Five times he made unassisted double plays by grabbing low liners on the first hop and then stepping on second base and throwing to first.

When does a Speaker not speak? Tris Speaker and Duffy Lewis didn't speak to each other for years after the day Lewis threw a bat at Speaker and hurt him; the balding Lewis was reportedly angry at Speaker for pulling his cap off during batting practice.

S peaking of Speaker, he started his career as a pitcher but moved to the outfield to take advantage of his talents as a hitter, foreshadowing Babe Ruth's similar migration from the mound to the outfield. Cy Young used to hit him fungoes every day to help him develop his fielding, and Speaker always credited Young for the help. Speaker seemed to have a number of talents. One day, he bested Will Rogers during a roping exhibition put on before a benefit game for a Boston sportswriter's widow.

Tracy Stallard

A fter Roger Maris hit his then-record 61st regular-season home run off Red Sox Tracy Stallard, the rookie pitcher was besieged by reporters' questions. "I have nothing to be ashamed of," he replied. "He hit 60 others, didn't he?"

Bob Stanley

I n 1986, reliever Bob "Steamer" Stanley was going through a rough time. Cursed with a sinkerball that no longer sunk, he was booed mercilessly by the Red Sox fans but still managed to keep his sense of humor. He told teammates that his actual name was Lou Stanley and that actually fans were chanting "Lou, Lou," when he walked to the mound.

W hen "Steamer" prowled the home bullpen in the late 1980s, he developed a great rapport with the fans—the infamous "bleacher creatures." Anytime a beach ball landed on the field, Stanley would ceremoniously place the ball on the ground and, as if performing a sacred sacrifice, use a ground crew rake and pop the ball, throwing the deflated remains back to the cheering bleacherites.

S tanley was very active with the Jimmy Fund and did his best to brighten the lives of children stricken with various forms of cancer. "One time, I went to visit this boy who wouldn't come out of his room because they had taken his eye out. I brought him one of my jerseys from the 1983 season when I had set the Red Sox record with 33 saves. I also brought him a bat and a ball, and I gave them to him, and we talked for awhile. When I got home, the doctor called. 'I don't know what you did, but he's running down the hallway with your jersey as a night shirt.' He was only 10, and the thing was down to his feet. A couple of weeks later, I ran into his father, who was a security guard at the racetrack. I asked him about his son, and he told me that he had died. He said they had buried him with my jersey." After Stanley retired in 1989, his own nine-year-old son, Kyle was diagnosed with a similar kind of cancer. Kyle recovered due to advances made in those few intervening years—advances made in no small part due to the wonderful work of the Jimmy Fund.

Stealing Home

The Pawtucket Red Sox, the top minor-league affiliate of the parent Boston Red Sox, hosted the longest game in baseball history: a record 33-inning marathon against the Rochester Red Wings. The game began on April 18, 1981, and continued for eight hours, well into the morning of April 19, when it was finally called with the score tied 2-2. When one of the Pawsox players returned home in the wee hours of the morning of April 19, his wife was justifiably suspicious and demanded an explanation. The exhausted and bedraggled player pleaded innocence, explaining that he had been playing baseball until a few minutes previous. His wife remained skeptical until he showed her the morning newspaper featuring front-page accounts of the game. The grueling contest was eventually concluded on June 23.

The game finally ended when Marty Barrett scored on a Dave Koza hit to give the Red Sox a 3-2 victory. Koza went 4-for-13 in the contest. Future Boston Red Sox star and 3000-hit third baseman Wade Boggs managed 4 hits in 12 trips to the plate, while future Orioles iron-man Cal Ripken Jr., playing third for Rochester, went 2-for-13.

This game established more records—and created more trivia questions—than many entire seasons. Here are some of the 14 records set in this marathon: Most innings: 33; most putouts, one team: 99 (Pawtucket); most putouts, both teams: 195; time: 8:25; most strikeouts, one team: 34 (Rochester); most strikeouts, both teams: 60; most pitches thrown: 882 (423 by Rochester; 459 by Pawtucket); most at-bats: 14 (Dave Koza, Lee Graham, Chico Walker).

Vern Stephens

In 1953, during batting practice at Fenway, St. Louis Browns shortstop Billy Hunter stroked a line drive that hit a pigeon in center field. The pigeon fell to the ground but quickly recovered and flew off, prompting Red Sox shortstop Vern Stephens to comment: "That's a sure sign, Billy. When you can't knock out a bird with a line drive, it's time to start looking for another job."

Junior Stephens was a free spirit but a dedicated ballplayer. The night before a twin-bill in Cleveland, some mobsters tried to get him drunk in order to influence the outcome of the games. After a night of carousing with his newfound friends, Stephens hit three home runs and drove in 11 in the next day's doubleheader, foiling the plans of the gamblers.

Dick Stuart

If any man was born to be a designated hitter, it was Dick Stuart, alias Dr. Strangeglove and the Boston Strangler. Unfortunately, Stuart came along before the DH rule came into effect in the American League. Stuart possessed amazing power and could win a ballgame with a single swing of the bat. He also was a threat to give up as many runs as he produced. The kindest description of his play at first base is erratic. Even Hank Aaron addressed him as "Stonefingers," and it was rumored that his glove was not made by Spalding or Rawlings but by the Portland Cement Company.

His defensive technique was sometimes referred to as the "¡Olé!" approach—he waved his glove at the ball as it passed by, like a matador with his red cloth. One day, after yet another miscue had led to yet another opposition score, Stuart was given a standing ovation at Fenway for successfully scooping a hot dog wrapper that had blown across the infield.

Before he came to the Red Sox, Stuart played for the NL's Pittsburgh Pirates. One day, the announcer gave the usual pre-game announcement to the Forbes Field crowd: "Anyone who interferes with a ball in play shall be ejected." The Pirates' beleaguered manager Danny Murtaugh grumbled to no one in particular: "I hope Stuart doesn't think that means him."

Not only was Stuart inept as a fielder, his base-running skills also left much to be desired. He was always missing or misreading his coach's signs. He once suggested: "When I get on base, why not just point to the base you'd like me to go to?"

The press loved Stuart because he provided great newspaper copy. Once, at a Boston post-season baseball banquet, he got up to speak and noted that his manager Billy Herman was in the audience. "Hope you have a great winter, Billy," said Stuart as Herman nodded his thanks. "Because you had a horseshit summer," he continued after a short pause.

Dick Stuart

S tuart was once stopped by a Boston police cruiser. The officer pointed out that Stuart still had 1963 license plates on his car despite the fact that it was now 1964. "I had such a good year that I didn't want to forget it," he explained.

D ick Stuart, who hit 66 HRs one year in the minors, is the only first baseman in major-league history to have three assists in one inning. Dr. Gold Glove, perhaps? More like Dr. Jekyll.

George Thomas

R ed Sox utility man George Thomas (1966-71) was no Ted Williams. He finished his 13-year major-league career with a .255 batting average and a paltry 46 homers. In 1970, he got a rare starting assignment and responded with three doubles. When reporters gathered around his locker after the game, he deadpanned: "I'm exhausted. Please tell (manager Eddie) Kasko that he can either bench me or trade me."

Luis Tiant

"Luis Tiant is the Fred Astaire of baseball."–Reggie Jackson

Red Smith once described Luis Tiant as follows: "He is a joy to watch; this swarthy, ample gentleman of 34 going on 44. Black-bearded and sinister, he looks like Pancho Villa after a tough week of looting and burning. He is a master of every legal pitch, and he never throws two consecutive pitches at the same speed." One of the most enduring images for Red Sox fans is that of Luis Tiant in the middle of his corkscrew delivery: back to the batter, eyes rolling skyward as if seeking divine intervention. As Joe Garagiola once said; "How can you hit a guy who doesn't even look at you when he goes into his wind-up?"

Luis Tiant's father, also named Luis, was considered one of the greatest pitchers in Cuba's storied baseball history. He had pitched against and defeated several touring major-league teams. The younger Tiant pitched for a year in the Cuban League in 1960-61, then he left revolutionary Cuba for Mexico and eventually the United States, never to return to his native land. Luis Sr. had never seen his son take the mound in the major leagues, but in 1975, Fidel Castro gave him special dispensation to visit Boston, where he threw out the first pitch at a game late in August. It was the first time father and son had seen each other in eight years. When his first attempt was a little low and outside, he motioned for the ball again and the old man fired a perfect strike right over the plate. Luis Tiant Sr. and his wife both passed away that winter.

An avid fisherman, Carl Yastrzemski once brought a prize catch into the Red Sox spring training clubhouse in Florida to show it off. Predictably, Luis Tiant saw an amazing resemblance between the fish and his favorite target, Tommy Harper. "It's got teeth like Harper's," he shouted gleefully. Later, when the unsuspecting Harper entered the clubhouse, he was greeted with a stony silence. Spotting his Red Sox uniform on the floor by his locker, he bent to pick it up. To his surprise, a large and rather ugly fish was already "wearing" it, its grinning mouth propped open with tongue depressors and a Red Sox cap atop its head.

Stopped for speeding by a Massachusetts state trooper, Tiant explained to the officer, "I was bringing some heat." The cop, obviously a Red Sox fan, let him off without a ticket.

For the entire 1974 season, Luis wore nothing but white, save for his Red Sox uniform. He said it was his personal tribute to God.

Pitchers are especially notorious for their superstitions. Luis Tiant used to smoke cigars in the shower after a game. Boston's one-time pitching coach Lee Stange claimed that Tiant also wore strands of beads and a special loincloth that he wrapped around his waist under his uniform to ward off evil spirits.

Tiant was obviously a cock-eyed optimist. Steve Dillard recalls him in spring training one year, after someone had smashed one of his pitches to straight-away center field, yelling: "GO FOUL! GO FOUL!"

Bill Lee, himself no stranger to humor, claims: "Luis Tiant was by far the funniest guy I ever played with. He just had an uncanny sense of humor with his broken English and the way he expressed himself. He and Tommy Harper just kind of went back and forth with each other. He'd call Harper 'liver lips,' and he'd bring in a picture of a big-lipped chimpanzee, and he'd look at it and say: 'I love you, Tommy.'

"Whenever he went in to take a shit, he'd flush the toilet and say: 'Goo bye Tommy!' They were just at each other's throats all the time."

After weeks of the "Goo bye Tommy!" stuff, Harper finally struck back. Tiant was always on guard while he was in the bathroom stall, apprehensive after playing so many tricks on others. One time, Yaz noticed Luis wasn't as vigilant as usual and helpfully alerted Harper, even supplying a bucketful of cold water. Harper climbed up onto a sink, walked along the row

Luis Tiant

of sinks and positioned himself perfectly. When the flush began and Tiant was in the middle of his "Goo bye Tommy!", Harper suddenly poured the full bucket over Luis, to the delight of the 23 other players who had gathered to watch the drama unfold.

Like many baseball couples, Tiant met his wife Maria at the ballpark—but in this case, he was the fan, and she was the player. On an off night in Mexico City where he was playing for Los Tigres on his way from Cuba to the majors, he attended a girls softball game and was smitten with the attractive left fielder.

John Valentin

Besides being a steady third baseman and a fine clutch hitter, John Valentin is the Red Sox player currently most active with the Jimmy Fund. John's agent concedes that it was originally a self-serving strategy to assist him in salary arbitration, but the more he became involved with the kids, the more he wanted to contribute to the cause. When a young cancer patient named Lucas Bartlett expressed a Christmas wish to meet Valentin, John and his wife Marie agreed to stop by for a few minutes. The few minutes turned into four hours and regular contact until the boy's death the following August. For the rest of the season, Valentin wore Lucas' name in his cap and has worked to preserve his young friend's memory through various noble deeds.

The 1999 American League Divisional series pitted the Cleveland Indians against the Boston Red Sox. The Sox lost the first game in Cleveland 3-2 when ace starter and shoe-in for the Cy Young Award Pedro Martinez was forced from the game with a pulled back muscle. Game Two was even worse as the Sox were unraveled by the Indians 11-1.

Back in Boston for Game Three, the Red Sox finally came alive, winning 9-3. Game Four was even better as the Sox massacred the Indians 23-7 to set several post-season records for runs scored. John Valentin had alternated between hero and goat in the first three games, committing egregious errors and hitting dramatic home runs. In Game Three, he made a costly throwing error only to redeem himself with a game-winning homer. Tapping into recent Red Sox history, Fox sports announcer Bob Branley commented that Valentin had gone "from Bill Buckner to Carlton Fisk in a single game."

John Valentin

Before Garciaparra arrived in Boston, Valentin was the regular Red Sox shortstop. If ever there was cause for dissension in the ranks, this surely offered that potential. The Boston media sharpened their pens to record the gathering storm. So how do the two infielders get along? "I love the guy," says Nomar. "He's taught me so much about playing shortstop and about playing baseball. People would naturally think he'd be the last one to help me. There is just one word to describe John: class. A complete class guy. He's always been that way to me. We've gotten really close, and we're great friends."

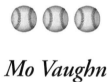

Mo Vaughn

The "Hit Dog" was one of the most active Red Sox players ever in the Greater Boston community and founded the Mo Vaughn Youth Development Center, which has helped significant numbers of inner city kids. Brian Wilson, a childhood friend of Mo's since age 9, heads the Center. Mo's parents were often seen at Fenway. Both are teachers, and his father is also a school principal.

While with the Red Sox, Mo befriended young Jason Leader, a Jimmy Fund patient seriously ill with cancer. The boy asked Mo to hit a homer for him, and Mo said he'd try. That day, he did hit one and made all of Boston—and especially one young boy—happier for one day. Jason later died, but Mo, his parents and the Leaders have maintained an on-going friendship.

Mickey Vernon

Mickey Vernon and Ted Williams had parallel careers. Vernon entered the major leagues with the Washington Senators in 1939, the same year that Williams arrived in Boston, and they both retired from the game in 1960. The two great hitters were teammates on the Red Sox in 1956 and 1957. "It was a thrill for me to play with Ted," says Vernon. And much safer than playing against him, adds the former first baseman and two-time AL batting champ. "I hated playing first when Ted was at the plate because he pulled everything. You don't want to be holding someone on base when he's up—and the Red Sox always had someone on base. DiMaggio and Pesky hit ahead of him, and they were good hitters, and they'd either walk or get a hit and be on base every time. Once he crushed a sinking line drive at me and I flipped my glove down in front of my crotch, and the ball had so much topspin on it, it went right up between my legs."

During the Second World War, Vernon was stationed on the tiny South Pacific island of Ulithi, which was a mile long and a quarter of a mile wide. Also stationed there were future Red Sox star Billy Goodman and the great Larry Doby, giving Ulithi more talent per square mile than any other atoll on earth. "We didn't have room to play baseball, so we played softball," says Vernon.

"Broadway" Charlie Wagner

Superstition has always been a great part of baseball. When a team is going well, no one wants to be responsible for breaking the spell. In 1938, the Red Sox were on just such a winning streak, and players went to extreme measures to keep it going. During the eight-game run, the team was served lamb chops every day. Joe Cronin chewed the same gum throughout the streak, and other players tried to maintain their regular eating routines. Perhaps it was Wagner who made the biggest sacrifice for the team. "I was on prune juice for eight straight days," he claimed. "I'm glad we lost."

Y ou don't often hear of a player asking to be sent from the big leagues to the minors, but that's exactly what Charlie Wagner did in 1938. Starting the season with the Red Sox, he wasn't getting any playing time and felt that his skills were diminishing as a result. He went to manager Joe Cronin and demanded a demotion. "You can't watch people play," he says. "You've got to play in order to learn and not get stale." The Red Sox obliged and sent Wagner to Minneapolis, where he developed a friendship with a promising young outfielder named Theodore Williams. The next year the two were roommates with the Red Sox.

W agner was Ted Williams' first roommate and tells many stories about the times he'd wake up to find Ted swinging an imaginary bat in the room— checking his swing in the mirror. One morning, Ted used a real bat and inadvertently smashed Wagner's bedpost, breaking the bed and waking up the man they called "Broadway" beause of his natty attire. Now in his late 80s, Wagner is a Red Sox staffer at spring training every year. He even has a street named after him in the Red Sox complex at Fort Myers. Is that Broadway . . . or Wagner Way? (Actually it's Charlie Wagner Way.)

John Wasdin

Nomar Garciaparra hit his first major league homer off John "Way Back" Wasdin. "It's a funny story because I didn't know who I hit it off until John was traded to the Red Sox. I don't really know pitchers. I found out in spring training that it was Wasdin. He had just come over to our team, and I didn't know him. We were all doing our stretching exercises, and he came up to me and said: 'You know, you haven't even thanked me yet.' And I go: 'For what?' And he said: 'I got your career started.' Then we just laughed. He's a really good guy and we became very good friends. I just said: 'Alright! Thank you!' Even to this day, we'll joke around. He'll say to everyone: 'You know who got Nomar started, right?' I'll say: 'It was John Wasdin, right here. If it wasn't for him, I don't know where I'd be.' "

Sammy White

This story comes from the "true or falsie" department. Parnell claims that White had some rather unconventional catching equipment. "Sammy used to use a woman's falsie as a sponge in his glove. When you think about it, it is the ideal thing because it fits the hand perfectly and creates that air vacuum between the rubberized sponge and the glove, which would soften the impact of the ball hitting in his glove. One day, he goes over to the wall after a foul ball and hits the wall, and the glove flies off, and darned if the falsie doesn't land in a girl's lap. She was so embarrassed; she thought people would think it was hers. Her face was as red as can be. Everyone wanted to laugh but they couldn't. It took Sam to think of that."

Mickey McDermott has another true falsie story about Sammy White. "Sammy goes into a department store, and he see these falsies in a barrel. He says to the lady clerk: "What size do you have there?" She said: "You mean for your girlfriend?" He said: "No, for me." She said: "Oh, my God!" He buys two of the falsies and painted the nipples red, and they fit between his two fingers perfectly and when they were doubled up they made a great sponge for this catcher's mitt—because when you set down and catch fastballs all day long, your hand gets killed. We didn't have those big padded gloves in those days. Well, there was a close play at home plate one day where the lead runner from third was coming home and the anchor runner is coming around third and almost catches the lead runner. It should have been a sure double play—bang bang—at home plate for Sammy. As he tags one, the other runner hit him, and his glove flew off, and there were the two big shiny tits with bright red nipples lying in the middle of the field. The place went nuts. They thought he was a cross-dresser and they'd knocked his bra off or something, that he didn't have a chest protector, he had a bra on. Sammy had a locker full of those things."

Dick Williams

Williams was the acerbic manager of the 1967 Red Sox, transforming the team that had finished in ninth place the previous year into the Impossible Dream pennant winners. Lacking any discernible diplomatic skills, he didn't make many friends in the process. He told Joe Foy that he was so fat he couldn't bend over for a ground ball. He was equally critical of George Scott's eating habits and had nothing much good to say about benevolent Red Sox owner Tom Yawkey, making Williams perhaps the only person in his employ ever to criticize the likeable owner.

Ted Williams

"Ted has conquered the air because he's been an ace pilot; he's conquered the sea because he's caught so many fabulous

fish; and he's conquered baseball. I mean, what he needs is another planet." – Maureen Cronin

He was a hit in Boston before he ever set foot in that often-cynical town—this tall, skinny, 147-pound kid from San Diego. Early newspaper copy about him had whetted the New England appetite for a latter-day Moses to lead them from their baseball wilderness, another Babe Ruth to replace the one sold into bondage with the hated Yankees. When he arrived at his first spring training, teammate Bobby Doerr took young Teddy Williams aside and in hushed, almost reverential tones said, "Wait until you see Foxx hit!" Instead of being impressed, the Kid's off-hand reply was, "Wait until Foxx sees ME hit!" Ted Williams downed milkshakes to put on weight, smiled easily and positively bristled with self-confidence. He was a wild, fun-loving, clean-cut kid who'd shout at the bad guys in the movies and had been known to fire his shotgun out of a speeding car on the plains of Minnesota. His sole ambition was to walk down the street and have people say: "There goes the greatest hitter who ever lived." On dusty small town roadways, bustling city sidewalks and today's information superhighway, people have been doing just that for the last half-century.

Williams always had a keen eye. When he returned to Fenway for batting practice after being mustered out of the service mid-way through the 1953 season, he had been away from baseball for over a year. He stepped into the box for batting practice, took a few swings and then stepped out and asked what they'd done to the plate while he was away. No one knew what he was talking about. "It's out of line," he said. "You're nuts," was the reply. Williams insisted, measurements were taken and—sure enough—the plate was about one-quarter-inch out of alignment.

Ted was always a favorite of umpires. The general consensus among them was that if Ted didn't swing at a pitch, it must not have been a strike.

oston Herald writer Tim Horgan once interviewed a blind man who'd come to a Red Sox game and asked him why he didn't just stay at home and listen to the play-by-play on the radio. "I can tell when Ted comes out of the dugout," the man said, "then when he comes to the plate—just by the crowd reaction. There's no other player like Ted."

Had Ted not lost nearly five prime seasons to military service in World War II and Korea—having been called up the second time at age 34—projections show him hitting 701 home runs. If the competitive Williams had gotten that close to Babe Ruth's record, one can bet he would have found a way to hit 14 more before retiring.

Although writers were Ted Williams' sworn enemies, he still managed to inspire many a Boston columnist to literary flights of fancy. When he committed an error in left field one fine afternoon at Fenway, he was booed enthusiastically by Boston fans. When he homered later in the same game and was cheered by these same fans, it was more hypocrisy than Ted could stomach. He showed his contempt by spitting toward left field, then right field and finally toward the press box. One scribe, carried away by the exhibition, referred to Williams' performance as his Great Expectorations.

In Game Three of the 1946 World Series, Joe Garagiola had four hits and drove in three runs to lead the St. Louis Cardinals to a 12-3 victory over the Red Sox at Fenway Park. The next morning, the proud catcher rushed down to his hotel lobby to buy the morning newspaper, anxious to see how the Boston press had heralded his heroics. Much to his chagrin, the head-line read: WILLIAMS BUNTS!

When Teddy Ballgame was inducted into the National Baseball Hall of Fame, he wrote out his own speech the night before. It was an impassioned plea for recognition of the great Negro ballplayers who'd been excluded from the Hall of Fame only because the color barrier had kept them out of the big leagues for so long. "A chill goes up my back when I think I might have been denied this if I had been black," Ted said five years later in a speech at Howard University.

Ted Williams was a hero to fans and an idol to fellow hitters, but he was looked on with awe by big- league pitchers. Rookie pitcher Pedro Ramos once struck Ted out and then had the gall to enter the Red Sox dugout and ask the Splendid Splinter to autograph the ball used to strike him out. "Get the hell out of here!" roared Terrible Ted. "I'm not signing any ball I struck out on." Ramos, who idolized Williams, was crushed and tears welled in his eyes. Seeing this, the great Williams relented. "Give me the damn ball, and I'll sign it," he said. During the next Red Sox homestand, Ted once again faced Ramos. This time he tore into the pitcher's first offering and drove the ball deep into the right-field bleachers. As he trotted around the bases, he turned to the pitcher and shouted: "Go find that SOB, and I'll sign it for you too."

On July 14, 1946, the Boston Red Sox and Cleveland Indians met for a doubleheader at Fenway Park. In the first game, Ted Williams feasted on Indian pitching, hitting three home runs as the Red Sox won the marathon contest 11-10. Between games of the doubleheader, Williams decided to reward himself. When the last out had been recorded, he slipped through the door in the left field scoreboard and then through a trap door leading to the street. Still in full uniform, he walked to a nearby restaurant and placed his order: a large dish of ice cream. After consuming the frozen delight, Ted paid his bill, trotted back to the ballpark and emerged once again in left field, refreshed and ready for the remainder of the afternoon.

Ted's devastation of the Indians in game one had been so complete that it inspired Indians player-manager Lou Boudreau to introduce the infamous "Boudreau Shift," also known as the "Williams Shift." In Ted's first at-bat in game two, he doubled home three runs. Boudreau, who had watched his own record four doubles and a homer in game one go to waste, was so disgusted that he decided drastic measures were called for. He knew that lefty Ted was a dead pull hitter to right, and therefore he positioned his fielders on the right side of the ballpark.

If Fenway had been a ship it would have capsized to starboard. The first baseman and the right fielder were hugging the right-field foul line. The center fielder moved to deep right-center. The second baseman played a shallow outfield position, closer to first than to second, while the shortstop moved into the vacated second base position. The third baseman was in foreign territory directly behind second. Only the left fielder remained more or less true to Abner Doubleday's original concept, positioning himself in shallow left center field. Ted grounded out to Boudreau in his next at-bat and walked twice. Williams was to be faced with variants of the Shift throughout his career, stubbornly refusing to compromise his hitting principles by going to left field.

The Williams Shift was sometimes carried to ridiculous extremes. During a spring exhibition in Dallas in the late fifties, the manager of the opposing team placed all three outfielders in the right-field stands when Ted Williams came to the plate.

In early spring 1946, an agent of the Mexican Baseball League made a blatant attempt to coerce, cajole and entice Ted Williams into jumping from the majors to the Mexican circuit. Through an interpreter, he promised that Williams could "name his own figure and his own terms." The agent threw out a figure of $300,000 for three years. He told Ted that the right-field fences were short in Mexico and that the wind was always blowing toward the outfield. Williams appeared to be weakening. He squinted at the agent and asked: "Have you signed Bob Feller yet?" The agent asked why he wanted to know about the American League's best pitcher. "Well, if you've got Feller," said Williams: "I think I'll stay in the American League."

On June 9, 1946, Joseph A. Boucher was seated in row 33, deep in the Fenway Park bleachers, watching the second game of a double-header between the Boston Red Sox and the Detroit Tigers. It was a beautiful day for baseball, with the wind blowing out, although the bright sun made it difficult for fans in the bleachers to look toward home plate. Boucher heard the public address announcer introduce the next batter: Ted Williams. Then he heard the crack of the bat and the roar of the crowd, so he knew something significant was happening. However, not until Ted's home run drive had landed on the top of his head, denting his straw hat, did Mr. Boucher realize that he had become a footnote in Red Sox history. The drive was measured at 502', and today that seat has been painted red—standing out like a beacon in a vast sea of green. "They say it bounced a dozen rows higher, but after it hit my head, I was frankly no longer interested," admitted Mr. Boucher.

Ted Williams hit 12 home runs off Detroit's Virgil Trucks—more than he managed against any other pitcher. Trucks recalls his first encounter with his nemesis: "I will never forget watching Ted take batting practice during my first trip to Fenway Park in 1942. He was hitting the ball over the fences in the deepest parts of the ballpark. Unfortunately, when the game started—with me on the mound for the Tigers—he must have thought I was still pitching batting practice. In fact, everyone on the Red Sox seemed to be under that impression that day. The first batter hit a single on the first pitch; the second batter hit the first pitch for another single. Then up comes Williams. He smoked the first pitch for a double. With that, our manager, Steve O'Neil, came to the mound and so did my catcher, Bob Swift. O'Neil said to Bob: 'Doesn't Virgil have it today?', and Swift replied: 'How the hell would I know; I haven't caught a ball yet!'"

When Robert Redford played Roy Hobbs in the movie *The Natural,* he modeled his character after his hero: Ted Williams. He wore number 9 and tried to imitate Ted's swing. Redford explains: "The spirit and courage that Williams epitomizes was the guiding force behind my performance in *The Natural,* and I feel strongly that this performance was, in its way, my tribute to Ted." Why? "Any heroes I had when I was a kid were pretty much born out of reading Greek mythology. In real life, in real time, there was only one: Ted Williams. He was left-handed. I was left-handed. He was from Southern California, as was I. He was a baseball player. I wanted to be one when I grew up. Incidentally, I never achieved either objective."

In 1946, the All-Star Game was played at Fenway Park. To no one's surprise, Ted Williams stole the show. After homering early in the game, he came to bat in the eighth to face Rip Sewell, whose trademark was the so-called "eephus" pitch. Sewell threw the ball on a slow arc that reached a height of some 25 feet. No hitter had ever managed a home run against this blooper, and experts claimed that such a feat was impossible because the hitter had to supply all the power. When he stepped into the batter's box, Ted shouted to Sewell: "You're not going to throw me that #$@^% pitch— not in an All-Star Game?" Sewell grinned and nodded. The first offering was indeed the dreaded eephus, and after a moment of indecision, Ted swung and drove a vicious foul into the stands behind the third base dugout. The second pitch—another blooper—was outside. The one-and-one offering was a fastball, but Ted didn't bite. The Kid then proved the experts wrong. The next pitch, a classic eephus, floated slowly toward the plate like a deflating dirigible. Taking a single stride toward the ball, Ted drove it on a high arc into the right field bleachers. From their gleeful reactions, it was hard to decide who was most pleased—Rip or Ted. Today, Ted claims that if it had been a regular-season game, he would probably have been called out—he was two and a half feet out of the batter's box when he hit the ball!

Ted Williams, the man with the perfect baseball swing, was a mere mortal with a golf club in his hands. At the end of one particularly brutal round, the hitting perfectionist was so disgusted with his performance that he threw his clubs, bag and all, into a lake adjacent to the 18th hole. With a flurry of oaths disturbing the peaceful surroundings, he stalked to his vehicle only to discover that he had left his car keys in the golf bag.

Rolling up his pants legs, he waded into the pond and retrieved the bag. At this point, most people would have reconsidered their original rash act and cooled off. Not Ted. He retrieved his keys and promptly threw the clubs back in the water.

I t was the Splendid Splinter vs. Slammin' Sammy—a classic dispute between two legendary athletes over the relative difficulty of their respective sports. Golfer Sam Snead, possessor of perhaps the smoothest swing in golf history, and Ted Williams, the best pure hitter in the annals of baseball, were friends and fishing buddies. When it came to arguments, however, they both came out swinging.

Snead once visited the Red Sox dugout, where he and Williams discussed the merits of their two sports. "Golf's an old man's game!" taunted Williams, the ultimate needler. "You use a club with a flat-hitting surface and hit a ball that's not moving. In fact, it's teed up so that you can hit it better. On top of that, the galleries remain dead silent so as not to distract you. Meanwhile, I'm up there trying to hit a 100 mile-an-hour fastball or a curveball that looks like it's rolling off a table top. And at least half the time, a hostile crowd is yelling for me to strike out—and that's at Fenway Park!"

"Maybe so," said Snead, "but as a golfer I'm trying to get a ball in a four-and-a-half-inch cup. You're practically hitting into the whole world out there." "Not true!" countered Williams. "If I swing a split second too early, I pull it foul into the right field stands; too late, and I foul it into the left field stands." Snead paused for a moment before delivering the coup de grace. "Yes, Ted, but you don't have to wade into the stands to play your foul balls like I do." Williams' reply was not recorded.

" He took time off for the war to rest. I didn't have that opportunity. I had to stay and play . . . . I got tired."*–Bob Uecker, explaining why Ted Williams hit .344 lifetime with 521 homers, and he managed only a .200 average and 14 home runs.*

Ted quizzed everyone about hitting, even pitchers. "One day, Ted was about to bat against José Santiago," recalls southpaw ace Mel Parnell. "I was standing at the bat rack, and Ted asked me: 'What does this guy throw?' I went on to relate what I thought he threw and Ted said 'OK' and went up to the plate and hits the first pitch out of the ballpark. I said: 'Hell, you sure had a lot of confidence in a pitcher's opinion.' "

In February of 1994, Ted Williams, then 75 years old, suffered a serious stroke. Lying in a hospital and hooked up to an assortment of tubes and wires, Ted lapsed in and out of consciousness. He later told writer Dave Anderson about one particularly vivid dream; a dream that says it all about Ted Williams. As Ted tells it, he was half asleep and imagined he was back in spring training working with the young Red Sox hitters as he once did. Suddenly, fearsome left-hander Randy Johnson appeared on the mound, and the young Red Sox hopefuls were egging him on to hit against The Big Unit.

"I tell them: 'I haven't hit in years, and I just had a stroke, and I can't see too well,' but they keep teasing me and I say: 'Yeah, I'll do it.' But as I'm walking to home plate, I'm thinking: *I'm not going to try to pull this guy because he can really throw.* The first pitch he laid one right in there. I pushed at it. Line drive through the box for a base hit." Which only goes to prove what we already suspected: Ted Williams could hit today's pitching in his sleep!

Ted was apparently the last of the red-hot hitters. In a roundtable discussion organized by *Sports Illustrated* for an April 1986 cover story, hitters Ted Williams, Wade Boggs and Don Mattingly discussed the intricacies of their craft. Williams brought the conversation to an abrupt halt when he casually asked: "Have you ever smelled smoke from the wood burning on the bat?" Boggs was flummoxed at the very notion that such bat speed could be generated. Williams explained that five or six times in his career, he had faced good fastball pitchers and had just barely fouled the ball back, presumably causing the seam on the ball to burn. "That's the damnedest thing I've ever heard!" admitted Boggs, a future Hall of Famer.

Ted Williams was a hero to fans and an idol to fellow hitters, but he was looked on with awe by big- league pitchers. Satchel Paige was one of the best pitchers in baseball history, but, due to the color barrier, only fans of the Negro Leagues knew of his greatness. He finally made it to the Major Leagues when he was well past his prime but still more than a match for most hitters. In a key game during the hotly contested 1949 pennant race, the Red Sox faced Paige's Cleveland Indians. As the starting pitcher struggled, the 43-year-old Paige, as well known for his laid-back philosophy as for his superb pitching, warmed up alongside rookie reliever Mike Garcia. Paige, the elder statesman, tried to calm the nervous rookie.

"Those Red Sox don't have a hitter worth a moment's worry," soothed Satch. No sooner were the words out of his mouth than Boston's number nine hitter ripped a single to left. Leadoff hitter Dom DiMaggio then stepped to the plate. "DiMaggio is certainly not his brother. No sir, this is Dominic, not Joseph." DiMaggio promptly singled. Runners at first and second, no one out.

Johnny Pesky was next up. "He's a banjo hitter. All you have to do is pitch him around the knees," said Paige with a dismissive wave of his hand. Pesky lined a clean single to load the bases. As Ted Williams strode to the plate, the banter ceased, and Satchel grew uncharacteristically quiet. With the frenzied Fenway crowd roaring in anticipation, the Cleveland manager walked purposefully to the mound and signaled for Paige. Feeling like a man reprieved, Garcia waited for further words of wisdom from his guru, but none were forthcoming. Satch remained silent. Finally, he trudged from the bullpen with all the enthusiasm of a prisoner on death row. "One last thing, son," he drawled, rolling his eyes skyward. "When you're playin' these Red Sox, put your trust in the good Lord."

He was the Splendid Splinter, not a splendid sprinter, but Ted nonetheless set one speed record that still stands—although legitimate speedster Rickey Henderson duplicated it in the 2000 season. Ted was the only player in major league history to have stolen a base in each of four different decades. Williams had a lifetime total of just 24 stolen bases, but he spread them out efficiently: two in 1939, 14 in the 1940s, seven in the 1950s and one in 1960.

Only once did Ted Williams hit under .300. In 1959, suffering several injuries that limited his number of at bats to 272, Ted managed only .254. He decided to play one more year but stipulated that it would be on the condition that he be given a 30% pay cut. Ted felt he hadn't earned his salary. Owner Tom Yawkey reluctantly complied. There was no players'

union to argue that the best-paid hitter in baseball shouldn't be allowed to dock himself for a bad year.

Ted's Philadelphia Story

Ted Williams was a great hitter for many reasons: great eyesight, hard work, a will to succeed, and last but not least, his listening abilities. From his time in the minor leagues, right up through his entire major-league career, Ted sought out the Svengalis of swing and the high priests of hitting. He learned at the feet of Rogers Hornsby, Ty Cobb and Eddie Collins. He conferred with Bill Terry. He interrogated Collins about Shoeless Joe Jackson, Babe Ruth, Lou Gehrig and Cobb. Some of the advice he dismissed as incompatible with his own approach to hitting. Cobb's theories, for example, were completely foreign to Ted. Others he embraced, enhanced and added to his repertoire.

September 27, 1941 was a drizzly late summer evening in Philadelphia. It had rained hard earlier in the day, canceling the ballgame, and passersby rushed heads down along the tree-lined streets, scarcely noticing the tall athletic man and the shorter, stockier man walking along in animated conversation. Few of the onlookers were aware that the taller man was on the verge of a feat so rare that it has not been repeated in any baseball season since.

They walked through business areas and neighborhoods with immaculately manicured lawns. Occasionally, the shorter man would duck into a bar for a quick refresher, while the athlete went for ice cream.

The taller man, Red Sox phenom Ted Williams, and his less imposing friend, clubhouse boy Johnny Orlando, were talking hitting—specifically the next day's season- ending doubleheader between the Red Sox and the hometown Athletics. Ted reckons they walked about ten miles that night. Exactly what was said is long forgotten, but knowing Williams, he was analyzing the pitchers he would see the next day—what they might throw in particular situations and on specific counts.

The last time anyone had batted .400 was 1930, more than a decade earlier, when Bill Terry batted .401 for the National League's New York Giants. Terry had been the closest thing Ted had to a boyhood idol. The last American Leaguer to reach the mark was Harry Heilmann, way back in 1923. As he walked, Ted remembered the encouraging words he had heard from Heilmann a few weeks earlier: "Just hit the way you can hit, and you'll be all right."

Going into the twin bill, Williams was batting precisely .39955—which for math majors everywhere, and certainly by major league baseball standards, would make him a .400 hitter. But Ted's personal standards were even higher. He did not want to leave his fate up to the discretion of a statistician in some airless league office. Earlier that same evening, Sox manager Joe Cronin had suggested that maybe Ted would like to sit out the last two meaningless games to preserve the coveted mark. Ted's reply was as blunt as it was powerful. "If I can't hit .400 all the way, I don't deserve it," he said. There was no argument.

Ted Williams

Just before this crucial two-game finale, Al "Bucketfoot" Simmons, then a coach for the Athletics, swaggered into the Red Sox dugout, intent on planting doubts in the young hitter's mind. Four times in his career, Simmons, a lifetime .334 hitter, had averaged over .380, leading the American League in 1930 and '31. He and Cobb had always criticized Williams for being too selective at the plate. Approaching Ted, he taunted: "How much you wanna bet you don't hit .400?" Lesser men would have found the challenge from a bona fide Hall of Famer disconcerting, if not devastating. Not so Williams. If anything, it had the opposite effect, galvanizing Ted to the task at hand.

September 28 broke cold, damp and dreary at Shibe Park—the sort of day that signaled the imminent move from the diamond to the gridiron. The crowd of 10,000 who braved the unpleasant conditions was rooting for the kid from Boston. In fact, they were pulling for him all the way. As he entered the batter's box, he heard home plate umpire Bill McGowan mutter: "To hit .400 a player has got to be loose." Ted had always enjoyed a great relationship with umpires; he respected them and never showed them up, and they, in return, marveled at his uncanny knowledge of the strike zone.

Ted was undeniably loose. He singled sharply in his first at-bat, then homered to straightaway center field, and finished the game with two more singles and a walk. After game one, there was no way he could fail to hit .400, and many felt he would sit out the second game with a clear conscience. To the surprise and delight of the Philadelphia fans, however, Ted trotted out to his position in left field. In game two, he confirmed his legend by doubling off the loudspeaker in right field and adding another hit. At the end of the day, he had accumulated six hits in eight at-bats, raising his average to .406.

Heilmann had been right; Simmons dead wrong! Ironically, perhaps appropriately, in 1927, Heilmann had also battled down to the wire before capturing the American League batting title. Like Ted, he had refused to sit out the second game of a doubleheader to preserve his title. He picked up three hits to raise his average to .398 and win handily over the runner up—one Al "Bucketfoot" Simmons.

Jim Willoughby

"They never should have taken out Willoughby." Along with "They should have taken out Buckner!", "They should never have sold Babe Ruth!", and "They should never have started Galehouse," this statement ranks right up there as a hot-stove league perennial when discussing the great mysteries of Red Sox history. In Game Seven of the 1975 World Series, the Red Sox and Cincinnati Reds were tied 3-3 going into the ninth inning. Jim Willoughby, a willowy sinker-ball artist, had been brought on in the seventh and silenced the Reds' big bats, retiring Johnny Bench with the bases loaded. He then mowed down the Reds 1-2-3 in the eighth. But in the bottom of the eighth, with a runner on first and two out, manager Darrell Johnson pinch-hit for Willoughby, thereby removing Boston's best reliever from his arsenal. As every Red Sox fan knows, the Reds scored against his replacement, Jim Burton, in the top of the ninth and clinched the World Series.

Smoky Joe Wood

"Can I throw harder than Joe Wood? There's no man alive that can throw harder than Joe Wood." – Walter "Big Train" Johnson

Smoky Joe Wood's 1912 pitching record was an amazing 34-5—the best of the century with the possible exception of Walter Johnson's 36-7 slate in 1913. Wood recorded 258 strikeouts, a 1.91 ERA and 10 shutouts. He pitched 35 complete games and a total of 344 innings! On September 6, 1912, Wood and Johnson met in the most anticipated and hyped sporting event of the young century. To add to the drama, Wood was looking for his 14th consecutive win in front of the hometown crowd at Fenway Park. Johnson, known because of his blazing speed as the Big Train, had set the record earlier that same season when he won 16 straight. It was a promoter's dream; a match made in Cooperstown. It would be difficult to imagine a modern equivalent, but picture Roger Clemens in his prime taking the mound against Pedro Martinez, and you get some idea.

To say that the game was a pitching duel is like saying that Ali vs. Frazier was a mild disagreement. The two moundsmen did not disappoint the capacity crowd, throwing fastball after fastball past overmatched batters. Not until the bottom of the sixth inning did the Red Sox finally spoil the two neat rows of zeros on the scoreboard. With two men retired, Tris Speaker, Wood's best friend and roommate, doubled. Duffy Lewis followed with another double to score Speaker. Appropriately, the final score was 1-0, with Wood emerging victorious and winning his 14th in a row. He would go on to win his next two as well to tie Johnson's new American League standard.

Carl Yastrzemski

"I loved the game. I loved the competition. But I never had any fun. I never enjoyed it. All hard work; all the time." –Yaz

What's in a name? Carl Yastrzemski was so popular in Boston that Sherm Feller used to introduce him only by his number: "Number 8!" Only Yaz and Ted (# 9) have reached that numerical level of fame with the Red Sox.

Bill Lee suggests that Yaz's longevity had much to do with the number he wore: "When he lies in bed at night, it forms the algebraic symbol for infinity."

Like Ted Williams, his predecessor in left field, Carl Yastrzemski was often the target of abuse from the fans down the left field line at Fenway. He once turned the jeers into cheers by trotting to his position, and with great show, removed large wads of cotton from his ears.

In 1967, Carl Yastrzemski hit 44 homers, had 121 RBIs and a .326 batting average to win the Triple Crown—a feat that hasn't been achieved in either league since. He was named the American League MVP. More significantly, Yastrzemski led the Red Sox out of the baseball wilderness to their first American League pennant in 21 years. Ninth-place finishers the previous year, they had entered the campaign as 100-1 long shots, and even those odds seemed overly optimistic at the time. The Sox had languished in the doldrums for several years since Ted Williams retired, and interest in the team had faded. But in 1967, they caught fire, led by this Polish son of a Long Island potato farmer. Yaz did it all for the Red Sox that year. He hit for average, and he hit with power. He ran the bases with calculated abandon. He played left field like no one before or since. The Green Monster was his personal domain, and he used it to his advantage. There may have been better statistical years on paper—but Yaz came through in the clutch so many times, it was almost supernatural. His name was gold and suddenly everyone, even those who could spell little else, could spell it perfectly.

As the pressure-packed pennant race moved toward its climax, Yaz just got better and better, batting an astounding .523 in the last two weeks of the season. In the last two games of the season against Minnesota, he hit safely in seven of his eight trips to the plate, sealing two victories for the Sox and making the Impossible Dream a reality. In the '67 World Series, Yaz batted .400 in a losing cause, winning respect from both leagues and fans across America.

Carl Yastrzemski

Ted Williams once observed: "I never played with Yaz, but Bobby Doerr told me that in 1967 he had the best single year he ever saw, and Bobby played with *me* for 10 years! For that one year, he was Babe Ruth, Ty Cobb and Honus Wagner all rolled into one."

In the midst of the red-hot 1967 pennant race, Chicago White Sox manager Eddie Stanky questioned Boston's Carl Yastrzemski's baseball smarts, calling him "an all-star from the neck down." This psychological warfare gambit backfired. During the next series against the White Sox at Fenway, Yaz made several unbelievable plays in left field and went 6 for 9 at the plate. He put a giant exclamation point on the performance by homering and then tipping his hat to Stanky as he rounded third base. When he crossed home plate, Red Sox fans held a sign aloft that read: STANKY: A GREAT MANAGER FROM THE ANKLES DOWN.

Following his MVP performance in 1967, and a valiant effort in a losing cause in that year's World Series, Carl Yastrzemski was on top of the world. After being told how wonderful he was by everyone in Boston, even the usually humble Yaz was beginning to believe his press clippings. Until he went on a post-season Florida excursion with some friends, that is. Checking into the hotel, one of Yaz's friends asked if Mr. Carl Yastrzemski's room was ready. The clerk, obviously not a baseball fan, asked if he had a reservation.

After considerable ribbing from his companions, the group made its way to the room where a vase of flowers and a bowl of fruit awaited them on the dresser. At last, Yaz was getting the sort of respect he deserved, and he crowed to the others: "See, they do know me around here." Picking up the attached card, he read, to the vast amusement of all present: "Welcome, Charles Yastrzemski." Yaz says that even today, those friends call him Charles.

Williams, Foxx, Garciaparra, Yastrzemski

Yastrzemski holds the distinction of having played longer for one team than any other ballplayer. During his 23-year career with the Red Sox, he batted over .300 six times while playing under six U.S. Presidents. The *Boston Globe* pointed out that he reached that batting standard once during the presidency of John F. Kennedy, twice each while Lyndon Johnson and Richard Nixon occupied the White House, and once under Gerald Ford. Jimmy Carter and Ronald Reagan failed to inspire him to this level during their time in the office.

On September 12, 1979, Carl Yastrzemski made Red Sox and American League history by becoming the first player in the junior circuit to reach 400 homers and 3000 hits. He had achieved the 400 round-tripper milestone in July of '79. Hit number 3000 came off Yankee Jim Beattie, who as a boy growing up in the state of Maine had idolized Yaz.

In 1975, after striking out on a called third strike, Carl Yastrzemski showed his dissatisfaction with what he thought were repeated bad calls by umpire Lou DiMuro by scooping dirt into a large pile on home plate. He was quickly ejected from the game. "Yaz never thought an umpire had a right to call him out on strikes," recalls Bill Lee. "So he made a sand castle on home plate."

You've heard of giving a player a hotfoot? Renowned practical joker Carl Yastrzemski once carried the joke a bit farther north. He used newspapers to start a fire under unsuspecting teammate Doug Griffin's chair. While the rest of the team watched the conflagration grow, Griffin continued to read his newspaper, totally unaware of the flames lapping around him. Finally, the plastic chair got so hot that he shot out of it like a cannonball. Yaz was literally a pain in the ass.

" He was the worst dresser in baseball" claims Bill Lee.

"We called him Columbo, although he wasn't as sartorially attired. We tried to get rid of that damn raincoat. He must have had more than one. I remember once, he went into a slump in Minneapolis and at the hotel, he took all his clothes and set them on fire and called the fire department." On another occasion, Doug Griffin and Yaz were walking to the team bus, looking like two actors about to audition for the starring roles in *Dumb and Dumber*—Yaz had the entire back of his raincoat cut out, and Griffin was sporting trousers cut off at the knees.

Don Zimmer once sent Yaz a special delivery COD package. It cost Yaz $148 to find the box contained dead fish, dirt and rocks.

Tom Yawkey

Red Sox owner Tom Yawkey was often accused of running his team like a country club and spoiling his players. The truth is that Yawkey was the biggest Red Sox fan in town and wanted a winner more than anyone. He was a wealthy man with a down-to-earth approach to life. His generosity to his players went beyond money and was rewarded with a fierce loyalty seldom seen in today's game. When Mel Parnell pitched his no-hitter in 1956 at the age of 34, Yawkey was like a little kid. "When I got to the clubhouse, he was the first man to greet me," Parnell recalls. "He had a new contract and a pen in his hand and he said: 'Sign this!' I said: 'Mr Yawkey, you already pay me to do this kind of thing.' He said: ' Sign this already.' How many owners would do that? Not many."

His generous spirit was not confined to his ballplayers. Parnell remembers his love of kids and his love of the game. "Whenever we went away on a road trip, he'd work out at Fenway with Vince Orlando and take batting practice, and the kids around the neighborhood would go out and shag flies for him. When he was finished, he'd give them all a $20 bill. The kids loved that. He sent a lot of our batboys to college and one of them, John Donavan, came back to be our team lawyer."

Yawkey's highest paid ballplayer was Ted Williams, and while he was the most generous owner in baseball, his generosity did have limits. He could tolerate Williams offering hitting tips to players on second-division teams who were struggling, but when he saw him counselling the Yankees' young superstar Mickey Mantle, it was too much for even this kind man to bear. He asked Ted what the hell he was doing helping a hitter from the Red Sox' biggest rival.

Ted's reply says a lot about his love of the game. "T.A., just remember this: if you don't have any hitting in baseball, you don't have any excitement. When you're two or three blocks from a major league ballpark and you hear the crowd roar, somebody hit the ball! We've got to get more hitting in the game. Better backgrounds. So what if I help them a bit? It adds excitement to the game." Yawkey, who also loved the game above all else, agreed with his star.

Yawkey was beloved by his players because of his unassuming manner—a manner that included dressing very casually, certainly nothing like the sometimes- ostentatious owners of today. Sitting in front of his locker after a game one day, Bernie Carbo spotted his benefactor approaching. "Go get me a couple of cheeseburgers, would ya?" said Carbo. When Yawkey explained that he was the Red Sox owner, Carbo apologized. "I thought you were the clubhouse man," he explained sheepishly.

Bill Lee on Tom Yawkey:

"It was weird the day that Tom Yawkey died. There wasn't a cloud in the sky, and then he died, and right before the game a cloud passed over and delayed the game. It was kind of a homage to him. I was driving to the ballpark that day, and a pigeon stopped me going into the parking lot. I tried to pull to the left, and he walked to the left; I'd cut my wheels back to the right, and he'd move over that way. And he refused to let me go in there. I knew then that Tom Yawkey had come back as a bird because of all the DDT he had sprayed to kill spruce bud worms in his pine forests in South Carolina. In the process, he killed all the birds there. We'd talked about that, and I told him that he would have to do penance and come back as a bird. He was undergoing chemotherapy at the time. We got along great. Someone said that at the end of that ball game there was a pigeon that went up into the air and dove headfirst and committed suicide into the bleachers at Fenway Park. Even today, I'm always seeing Tom Yawkey out in the field. He's matriculated up. Now he's a crow."

Rudy York

Teammate Mel Parnell recalls Rudy York: "The big Indian led the league in burning up hotels. I think he set three hotels on fire. In my first year, 1947, I was rooming with Bob Klinger, and we could hear fire engines running around Kenmore Square like crazy, so we look out, and they're all going to the Myles Standish Hotel—a block away. When the fire was extinguished, the police brought Rudy over to our room at the Kenmore Hotel. We said: 'Rudy, what happened?' and The Chief says: 'I don't know. Some guy upstairs must have been smoking a cigarette, and he threw it out the window, and it blew in my window and set it on fire.' Actually, he had fallen asleep with a cigarette, and the next day the pictures of the ruined hotel room ran in the newspaper with bottles in sight on the dresser. So Mickey Harris cut the pictures out and put them by his locker. Rudy had a few choice words for him."

Rudy York was one of the few teammates to criticize the great Ted Williams. And he was man enough to do it to his face. In 1946, when the Red Sox were in hot pursuit of the American League pennant, York and some other Sox players felt that Ted hadn't hustled on a ball hit to left field. York confronted him in the clubhouse after the game. "We're about to win the pennant," York told him angrily. "Everybody's in this together. Anyone who loafs has got to answer to me." Williams took the criticism in the spirit it was intended, and the two teammates remained close friends. The Red Sox went on to win the '46 pennant.

Cy Young

Y is for Young,
The Magnificent Cy;
People batted against him,
But I never knew why.
—Ogden Nash

Cy Young is a name known to every fan of major league baseball. The award named for him is one of the most prestigious in sport and is synonymous with pitching excellence. Had the coveted award existed at the turn of the century, Young would have been a perennial candidate to capture it. Four times he won 30 games, and 15 times he won 20 or more. His final totals were 511 wins and 316 losses, with a lifetime ERA of 2.63. On May 5, 1904, the big right-hander (6'2", 210 lbs.) spun a perfect game against the Philadelphia Athletics—the first one since 1880. He struck out eight batters in a quick-paced contest that consumed only one hour and 20 minutes.

Cy Young

Matt Young

Matt Young proved to be a pretty disappointing pitcher for the Red Sox, averaging about five walks every game, and possessed a horrible psychological condition whereby he often could not throw the ball to first base, either on a bunt or a pick-off. He did have one moment, however, when the sun shone briefly through the clouds before becoming obscured once again. In a game against the Cleveland Indians in Municipal Stadium, Young pitched a complete game without allowing a hit. It wasn't ruled a no-hitter because the home team never batted in the bottom of the ninth —the Indians were ahead and won the game 2-1 in large part due to all the walks Young granted that day.

Norm Zauchin

What do you do with a caged bear? Norm Zauchin was up with the Red Sox for just five games in 1951, but then he had to go in the service. He made it back in 1955 and had his best year, contributing 27 home runs to the Red Sox cause. On State of Maine Day that season, three prizes were offered: Maine hens for whoever hit the first double in the game, Maine lobster for the first triple and a bear named "Homer" for the first home run. Zauchin had himself quite a day and won all three.

They didn't actually bring the bear to the park because they didn't know if anyone would actually win it. They shipped Homer from Maine to the zoo in Birmingham, Alabama. It grew old and eventually died there. The hens and the lobster were dispatched more quickly. There was just so much food that Zauchin brought them to the chef at the Somerset Hotel and hosted an elaborate party.

Don Zimmer

"If you can't play for Don Zimmer, you can't play for anybody." – Ted Williams

Though described as a "gerbil" by Bill Lee—who insists he did not mean it in an uncomplimentary fashion—Zimmer has had a remarkable baseball career as coach and manager and is well respected by many veterans. He had the misfortune to manage the Sox just at the time that many of them—the "Buffalo Heads"—were the most unmanageable.

With his old-fashioned attitudes, ample girth, bald head and the common knowledge that this head housed a steel plate from a past beaning, Zimmer was an easy target for ridicule. It was often said that he set off airport metal detectors. Zim soldiered on, but once or twice embarrassed himself and created additional fodder for Boston media long-hairs and young Turks. In 1976, he rushed out from the Sox dugout to argue a call, but tripped over first base and fell flat on the ground.

Don Zimmer

Don Zimmer sometimes treated his players with utter (or is that udder) disrespect. Speaking of his right fielder Dwight Evans, Zimmer once offered the following insights: "Next to Jim Rice, he's the strongest guy on the team—maybe in all of baseball—but he's got the balls of a female cow." And that's no bull.

Sadly, Zimmer was the Sox manager in 1978 when the team had built up a 14-game lead by the All-Star Game, only to see it completely erode and then had to struggle to force a one-game playoff. It was the so-called "Bucky Dent" game, in which the light-hitting Yankee hit a home run and broke countless hearts across the length and breadth of New England. In the spring of 1979 Don Zimmer and his wife were driving to Florida for spring training. It is reported that during the long drive, Zimmer would disturb extended periods of silence with the mumbled incantation: "Bucky Dent! Bucky ****ing Dent!"

BIBLIOGRAPHY

Berry, Henry. *Boston Red Sox* (Collier Books, 1975)

Blake, Mike. *Baseball Chronicles* (Cincinnati: Bitterway, 1994)

Boyd, C. Brendan and Fred Harris. *The Great American Baseball Card Flipping, Trading and Bubble Gum Book* (Warner Books, 1975)

Broeg, Bob. *Memories of a Hall of Fame Sportswriter* (Champaign, IL: Sagamore, 1995)

Cataneo, David. *Tony C* (Nashville: Rutledge Hill Press, 1997)

Clark, Ellery. *Boston Red Sox* (Hicksville, LI: Exposition, 1975)

Clemens, Roger with Peter Gammons. *Rocket Man* (The Stephen Greene Press, 1987)

DiMaggio, Dom with Bill Gilbert. *Real Grass, Real Heroes* (NY: Zebra, 1990)

Gammons, Peter. *Beyond the Sixth Game* (Houghton-Mifflin Co., 1985)

Golenbock, Peter, *Fenway* (NY: Putnam, 1992)

Harrelson, Ken and Al Hirshberg. *Hawk* (NY: Viking, 1969)

Hirshberg, Al. *The Red Sox, the Bean, and the Cod* (Boston: Waverly House, 1947)

Honig, Donald. *The Boston Red Sox: An Illustrated History* (Prentice-Hall, 1990)

Lautier, Jack. *Fenway Voices* (Camden, Maine: Yankee Books, 1990)

Lyons, Steve. *Psychoanalysis* (Champaign, IL: Sagamore, 1995)

Nowlin, Bill and Mike Ross with Jim Prime, *Fenway Saved* (Champaign, IL: Sports Publishing Inc., 1999)

Piersall, Jimmy & Al Hirshberg. *Fear Strikes Out* (Lincoln, NE: University of Nebraska Press, 1999)

Prime, Jim and Bill Nowlin. *Ted Williams: A Tribute* (Indianapolis: Masters Press, 1997)

Prime, Jim & Ted Williams. *Ted Williams' Hit List* (Indianapolis: Masters Press, 1996)

Reynolds, Bill. *Lost Summer* (Warner Books, 1992)

Sullivan, George. *Picture History of the Boston Red Sox* (Bobbs-Merrill, 1980)

Tiant, Luis and Joe Fitzgerald. *El Tiante* (NY: Doubleday, 1976)

Walton, Ed. *Red Sox Triumphs and Tragedies* (NY: Scarborough, 1980)

Walton, Ed. *This Date in Red Sox History* (NY: Scarborough, 1978)

Williams, Dick and Bill Plaschke. *No More Mr. Nice Guy* (San Diego, NY and London: Harcourt Brace Jovanovich, 1990)

Yastrzemski, Carl and Gerald Eskenazi. *Baseball, the Wall and Me* (NY: Doubleday, 1990)

Zingg, Paul J. *Harry Hooper* (Urbana: University of Illinois Press, 1995)

Our definitive statistical source was *Total Baseball,* edited by John Thorn and Pete Palmer